REFORM
AND
REFORMERS
IN THE
PROGRESSIVE
ERA

REFORM AND REFORMERS IN THE PROGRESSIVE ERA

**Edited by David R. Colburn
and
George E. Pozzetta**

CONTRIBUTIONS IN AMERICAN HISTORY, NUMBER 101

Greenwood Press
Westport, Connecticut • London, England

Library of Congress Cataloging in Publication Data
Main entry under title:

Reform and reformers in the progressive era.

(Contributions in American history, ISSN 0084-9219 ;
no. 101)

Bibliography: p.
Includes index.
Contents: Interpretations of twentieth century urban
progressive reform / Blaine A. Brownell — Al Smith and
the New York factory investigating commission, 1911-1915 /
David R. Colburn — Gino Speranza: reform and the immigrant / George E. Pozzetta —[etc.]
1. United States—Social conditions—Addresses,
essays, lectures. I. Progressivism (United States
politics)—Addresses, essays, lectures. I. Colburn,
David R. II. Pozzetta, George E. III. Series.
HN64.R422   306'.0973   82-6140
ISBN 0-313-22907-4 (lib. bdg.)   AACR2

Library of Congress Catalog Card Number: 82-6140
ISBN: 0-313-22907-4
ISSN: 0084-9219

First published in 1983

Greenwood Press
A division of Congressional Information Service, Inc.
88 Post Road West
Westport, Connecticut 06881

Printed in the United States of America

10 9 8 7 6 5 4 3 2 1

CONTENTS _____

INTRODUCTION

**David R. Colburn and
George E. Pozzetta**

The Progressive reform movement emerged at the turn of the twentieth century largely in response to the startling material changes and industrial developments taking place in American society. Its political roots intertwined in the Populist revolt of the late nineteenth century to which progressivism owed a great debt. Indeed, the earlier age provided the Progressive movement with many of its reform proposals. Unlike the farmers' revolt, however, progressivism received its principal support from urban voters on a national, not a regional scale. As noted by historians George Mowry and Richard Hofstadter, Progressive leaders tended to come from middle-class America, where education and social and cultural background clearly distinguished them from the Populists.

The central concern of the Progressive period was the relationship between government, business, labor, and the public. Much of the reform legislation of that era sought to guarantee federal and state protection for consumers and workers from ever-enlarging corporate power. Efforts to deal with concentrated monopolies differed substantially. Proposals varied from more stringent antitrust laws to labor welfare laws to consumer protection statutes. As George Mowry has written, "No general consensus was ever reached during the Progressive period ... except the proposition that an absolute private monopoly should not be permitted."[1]

The articles in this volume indicate the breadth and complexity of the Progressive movement. The authors point out that this reform wave involved more than just middle-class, white, Anglo-

Saxon Protestants; indeed, they suggest that progressivism touched the lives of Americans at all levels of society and of all persuasions.

These essays have attempted to portray more fully the Progressive experience and, perhaps in this manner, make it more comprehensible. The authors have examined individuals and groups not generally associated with the Progressive movement. What emerges from these articles is a multifaceted picture of progressivism. No one group or region was isolated from its influence. The authors have also demonstrated that the Progressive period remains a fertile area for study. Despite the excellent studies that have been written about this movement, more work remains to be done if the Progressive era is to be understood in its own right and in its relationship to the periods that preceded and followed it.

Blaine Brownell broadly discusses the twin issues of political reform and urban change in turn-of-the-century America. He approaches these themes through an examination of the various interpretations that have guided historians, observing that "there will doubtless never be universal agreement on the precise meaning of 'progressivism' and whether or not it was a distinct 'movement' or a vague collection of impulses for political change." Yet, Brownell posits the central importance of "groups, individuals, and activities usually grouped under the rubric of 'progressivism' " to the emergence of America as a modern state.

David Colburn reexamines the Triangle Shirtwaist Company fire and its impact on New York politics and on the political career of Alfred E. Smith. Colburn notes that the deaths of 143 young women in the fire served as a catalyst for a reform wave that rewrote factory legislation in the state. These reforms resulted from the investigations conducted over four years by the New York State Factory Investigating Commission and from the legislative leadership provided by Robert Wagner and Al Smith—two political stalwarts of Tammany Hall. Expanding on the thesis initially developed by J. Joseph Huthmacher and Nancy Joan Weiss, Colburn argues that the two men persuaded Tammany's leader, Charles F. Murphy, that it would be politically advantageous for the organization to mobilize its forces behind the factory reforms.

The boss played a crucial role during the Progressive period, serving as an urban power broker between the interests of the private and the public sectors. The massive growth of the city and the demands this growth generated on the city led to a breakdown of the traditional city-council government and to the emergence of the more efficient political machine. The boss assured local businessmen that their operations would not be jeopardized by local conditions and that lucrative city contracts were available to those who cooperated with the machine.

Al Smith's association with the Factory Investigating Commission exposed him for the first time to the hazardous conditions encountered by workers and to the ideas of reformers (especially settlement leaders) to alleviate these abuses. He became a prominent advocate of labor reforms and developed a close working relationship with New York's reform leaders while retaining his ties with Tammany Hall.

In his essay on the reform career of Gino Carlo Speranza, an Italian-American, a New York lawyer, and a spokesman for immigrant assistance, George Pozzetta seeks to portray the impact of progressivism on the immigrant community. Moved by the Progressive reform spirit and the problems faced by his immigrant brethren, Speranza worked closely with an organization to protect recent immigrants from those who sought to exploit them. Speranza's organization helped them find work, attend school, obtain legal assistance, and contact relatives.

Speranza hoped to bring an end to the padrone system, in particular, but failed because of the support the institution received from bankers, companies, and oftentimes the immigrants themselves. He also sought to rescue immigrant women from the evils of the sweatshop by opening a lace and embroidery school. The paradox of Speranza's career is that at the end of his life, he advocated the complete Americanization of all immigrants in America.

Judson Grenier assesses the relationship between the famous muckraker Upton Sinclair and his colleagues who played such an important role in inspiring Progressive reforms. Through personal interviews with Sinclair, Grenier finds that Sinclair differed from his colleagues in that he was younger, he approached his work in a more personal vein, and he was probably more ideologically committed than were other muckrakers.

Grenier also discloses that Sinclair had many disagreements with his fellow crusaders and felt that muckraking led to few significant reforms. Sinclair became disillusioned with the newspaper industry after several crusading journals compromised their efforts following pressures from advertisers and business managers.

Robert Vitz notes in his essay that the Progressive spirit made itself felt on the artistic community as well. Artists like Robert Henri and John Sloan of the Ash Can School assaulted the traditional academic painting in America, thereby transforming American art and preparing the way for the outburst of modernism.

Vitz writes that while they "paralleled Progressive reformers in their attack on the entrenched forces of artistic conservatism" and reflected Progressive concerns for urban society, they "only infrequently perceived of themselves as soldiers in the ranks of reform." Despite their talk about anarchism and socialism, Vitz suggests that their paintings of street scenes reveal "them, not so much as Socialists, as Jeffersonian Democrats."

In her article, Edwina Smith examines the impact of progressivism on Republican conservatism. She looks at the careers of two prominent Republicans from New England, George Hoar and Orville Platt, who served in the Senate for twenty-five years and who spoke for "principled political conservatism." Both men believed in progress and were optimistic about the future of the nation. Both also opposed extremism in any form. Platt frequently spoke out against the government's usurpation of the rights of the individual, while Hoar feared corporate monopolies and sought to curb their power through antitrust legislation.

Smith portrays the two men as centralizing conservatives who were ready to expand the role of the government for a variety of purposes, in contrast to several of their colleagues who opposed any role for the government in the economic sector.

Robert Rosenstone depicts the life of John Reed, who seriously questioned progressivism and the "bourgeois" world in which he was reared. Reed's father had actively supported Theodore Roosevelt and had led an environmental effort to save the Northwest timber lands. John Reed and his contemporaries, however, constituted a subculture that called "into question not only reform politics but the entire world view we term 'bourgeois.'"

Rosenstone contends that Reed and his peers differed with his parents' generation in absolutes, not in degrees. Reed scorned economic competition and material possessions; he sought, instead, a communitarian vision.

In the last essay, Keith Heim notes George Mowry's contribution to the profession and to our understanding of the Progressive era. He also reminisces about Mowry—the man and the historian. Heim lived at George Mowry's house in Chapel Hill, North Carolina, for four years during his graduate-student days and came to know him as few others did.

NOTE

1. George E. Mowry, *The Progressive Era, 1900-1920; The Reform Persuasion* (Washington, D.C.: American Historical Association, 1972), pp. 20-21.

REFORM
AND
REFORMERS
IN THE
PROGRESSIVE
ERA

1

INTERPRETATIONS OF TWENTIETH-CENTURY URBAN PROGRESSIVE REFORM

Blaine A. Brownell

In 1951, George E. Mowry sympathized with "the bewildered student of history [who] might well ask just who were the progressives, what prompted them to act, what they were trying to do, and where did they think they were going?"[1] These questions are perhaps even more pertinent thirty years later since the answers offered by a veritable legion of historians have been varied and even contradictory. Progressivism has been defined and redefined, examined and reexamined, with a fervor matched in few other areas of recent historical scholarship. George Mowry's work has been extremely significant in shaping this continuing investigation and in prompting much of the scholarly debate.

Mowry's study of *Theodore Roosevelt and the Progressive Movement* identified populism as the "real seedbed" of twentieth-century progressivism, and defined the national phenomenon in very broad terms:

> In its essence the progressive movement was a great social reaction against the preceding age. Compounded of moral, political, economic, and intellectual revolt, it was not restricted to one party but ran through the entire gamut of political organizations. Nor was it a product of a single economic class. Farmers and laborers were at its core, but they were soon joined by multitudes from the white collar and small business classes and even by some of the very rich. In fact, few reform movements in American history have had the support of more wealthy men.

It was this movement that in the course of fifteen years attempted, with a certain amount of success, to change the whole moral, economic, and political face of the country. Undoubtedly it altered the standards of political honesty and public morals. It inquired into the national structure of production and tried to redistribute wealth more equitably among all the nation's people. It made drastic changes in some of the old concepts of property which the race had held for centuries. It modified the organization of the American government as that government had not been changed since the Civil War. And, in not the least of its actions, it demonstrated that the federal government in the plentitude of its powers was the master of even the largest industrial combinations. One of the great accomplishments of the progressive movement was to fasten Jeffersonian idealism on a Hamiltonian structure in a partial realization of social democracy. Twenty years later another great reform movement was built upon that foundation.[2]

Mowry's focus in his earlier work was largely, of course, upon Theodore Roosevelt and the Bull Moose party of 1912, and thus, of necessity, upon ideology and politics. *The California Progressives* was a result of his conviction that "for real insight into the [progressive] movement one had to study it as it developed from the grassroots in the several states"[3]—a premise that was amply confirmed by the plethora of state and local studies that appeared soon thereafter. A chapter on "The Struggle for the Cities" recounted the efforts of "good government" forces to wrest control of Los Angeles and San Francisco from the tentacles of corporate domination and political corruption, and the extension of these efforts to the level of state government.

Mowry also attempted to identify more precisely the participants in that reform movement as a means of revealing its sources and motives. The "typical" California Progressive, he concluded, was young, well educated, a businessman or professional, with a midwestern and old-stock American background. This description was essentially extended to cover the national Progressive movement in *The Era of Theodore Roosevelt*, published in 1958, and was confirmed by other studies.[4] That such "fortunate sons of the middle class" would revolt against the status quo was largely attributable,

Mowry claimed, to the rise of the giant business corporation and the "rapid concentration of twentieth-century American life and its attending ethical, economic, and political manifestations," and to the increasing perceptions among members of the middle class that they were "hemmed in," their "place in society threatened by the monopolistic corporation on the one side, and by organized labor and socialism on the other."[5] Richard Hofstadter termed this a "status revolt" of older, established groups against threats posed both from above and below.[6]

Mowry's assessment helped to explain why well-to-do elements sought to gain a greater measure of control over their society and why they entered into the fray against the abuses of the giant corporations as well as against socialist radicalism and political corruption. But the challenges to that view of early twentieth-century reform emerged quickly and assumed a variety of forms. Gabriel Kolko was among the first to question the Progressives' commitment to social justice and economic reform. In *The Triumph of Conservatism*, Kolko argued that the nation's major economic interests guided and dominated politics during the Progressive era in order "to preserve the basic social and economic relations essential to a capitalist society, an effort that was frequently consciously as well as functionally conservative."[7] Rather than reducing the power of large corporations in any real sense, the reforms of the period served mainly to rationalize the economy in such a way that the larger corporations and financial institutions could function more securely and effectively. In Kolko's view, the Progressive era was misnamed: it consolidated the political control of dominant economic interests and witnessed a movement away from genuine political democracy.

James Weinstein provided further support for that view through his contention that a "liberal corporate social order" emerged in the first two decades of the twentieth century and persisted thereafter, a social order that was very different from the rising democratic tendencies of progressivism noted by Mowry and Hofstadter. Weinstein, if anything, carried the argument further by claiming that "liberalism in the Progressive Era—and since—was the product, consciously created, of the leaders of the giant corporations and financial institutions that emerged astride American society in the last years of the nineteenth century and the early years of the twentieth."[8]

Though their case clearly had merit, as subsequent studies would reveal, Kolko and Weinstein overstated a position—certainly in its most sweeping form—that was staked out more with assertion than with compelling evidence. The complexities of the period were shunted aside, and the roles and motives of numerous other groups were not explained. Their view had a greater implication of conspiracy by major economic interests than was justified, and it appeared as much a radical 1960s reaction to the weaknesses of liberalism as anything else.

Samuel P. Hays, though he did not adopt such a sweeping and roughly hewn notion of Progressive reform, nevertheless also questioned the "middle-class" character of progressivism and asserted that powerful elites were much more significant in the political changes of the period than was previously believed. Hays pointed to a number of studies that revealed that many opponents of Progressive reforms were also middle class in origin and status, and this seemed to undermine fundamentally the Mowry-Hofstadter thesis. Hays also noted the weaknesses of the middle-class distinction on other grounds: by the usual definition, middle class referred more to ideology and perception than to more objective social-class considerations, and its analytical usefulness was thus severely impaired. At the municipal level, Hays argued, political change was actually initiated and directed by upper-class individuals and groups rather than by the middle class.[9]

As middle-class Progressives were—in Mowry's view—buffeted by forces on either side, the prevailing historical interpretation of progressivism was similarly attacked. As Kolko, Weinstein, and Hays argued for the primary role of upper-class elites in Progressive reform, other scholars contended that lower-class groups were crucial. J. Joseph Huthmacher concluded that the political changes of the early twentieth century were the results of demands and initiatives rising from the lower classes, and he pointed to the role of foreign-born and working-class groups, especially in the cities, in creating an essential foundation for reform and a critical component of the political effort necessary to enact the Progressive agenda. John D. Buenker extended this approach even further in a series of essays examining a number of specific political changes and the importance of working-class and immigrant elements in bringing them about.[10] Both Huthmacher and Buenker emphasized the importance of broadly based coalitions in the political changes of the time rather than an exclusive focus on upper- or middle-class leaders and organizations.

David P. Thelen summed up a number of new ideas about progressivism and brought particular force to the notion that political coalitions were crucial. In a thoughtful article published in 1969, Thelen cited a number of works in addition to his own study of Wisconsin legislators and concluded that "the origins of progressivism cannot be found by studying the social background and tensions of progressive leaders." Simply stated, white, old-stock, middle-class business and professional people were just as likely to be conservative as progressive in their political persuasion and activity. Thelen traced the origins of progressivism back into the late nineteenth century as well, and suggested that it was born of the need somehow to confront and contend with the disastrous consequences of the economic depression of 1893, which were severe and dramatic enough to bring men and women of various opinions together in a common effort to restrain large economic monopolies and seek a greater measure of political democracy. In Thelen's view, the remarkable thing about the early twentieth century was not the class and status anxiety of certain groups, but the degree to which social tensions were held in check and various groups cooperated in order to achieve common objectives. "The basic riddle in progressivism is not," he wrote, "what drove groups apart, but what made them seek common cause."[11]

Perhaps the ultimate challenge to the Mowry-Hofstadter view of progressivism—and even to many of their critics—was Peter Filene's contention that progressivism was really no coherent "movement" at all by any reasonable social or ideological definition. "A diffuse progressive 'era' may have occurred," he suggested, "but a progressive 'movement' did not. 'Progressives' there were, but of many types—intellectuals, businessmen, farmers, labor unionists, white-collar professionals, politicians; lower, middle and upper class; southerners, easterners, westerners; urban and rural. In explaining American responses to urbanization and industrialization, these socioeconomic differences are more important than any collective identity as 'progressives.'"[12] The period from 1890 to 1920 was, according to Filene, much more ambiguous and shifting than previous interpretations had suggested. "Progressivism" was a label with little but convenience to recommend it.

The historical debate over progressivism—obituary or not—

continued, with different historians calling for more attention to religion, politics, or other aspects as keys to understanding reform in the early twentieth century. In 1977, three historians—John D. Buenker, John C. Burnham, and Robert M. Crunden—published in a single volume their various points of view on progressivism and their rejoinders to each other and to Filene's essay. Crunden even noted the often savage attacks upon the leading studies by Mowry and Hofstadter, and concluded that the "genuine insight and sophisticated intelligence displayed in these important studies often seemed to get lost in the quarrel about how, as it were, the sheep could be separated from the goats and accurately counted."[13] The debate had by no means come full circle; but the reactions to the Mowry-Hofstadter interpretation had gone in so many varying directions—and some so far—that efforts were already under way to assess the work that had been done and perhaps pull some of the threads together.

In one of the most sweeping and persuasive interpretations of the years from 1880 to 1920, Robert H. Wiebe saw the entire period as one characterized by the breakdown of local community autonomy and its replacement by a new social system "derived from the regulative, hierarchical needs of urban-industrial life."[14] Hundreds of "island communities"—the independent small towns of the nineteenth century—gave way increasingly in the 1880s and 1890s to a more nearly national society fashioned in more formal and bureaucratic terms. Within cities, the loosely connected neighborhoods became more interdependent through transportation improvements (especially the electric streetcar) and new central mechanisms demanded by rapid urban expansion. Farmers, laborers, and small entrepreneurs were affected more and more by the imperatives of the large corporation, and they often resisted. But a "new middle class," comprised of people with "strong professional aspirations" and also "specialists in business, in labor, and in agriculture awakening both to their distinctiveness and to their ties with similar people in the same occupation," found in the new changes, not a threat, but an opportunity.[15] This new middle class enhanced their identity by clustering in cities, especially in the industrial Northeast. In this largely urban arena, the various groups and factions either threatened or encouraged by change sought control over their lives and values.

Mowry gave substantial credit to populism for initiating challenges to the corporations and for promoting a greater measure of political democracy in the late nineteenth century. But he also emphasized the importance of municipal reform movements as an essential foundation for national political change. While many writers such as Huthmacher, Thelen, and Filene emphasized the diversity of reform—from farm to factory, and in all regions—the importance of political developments in the cities has been almost universally acknowledged, and has found special importance in Wiebe's interpretation. The processes of urbanization and industrialization were, as Mowry insisted, crucial in generating the conditions that set the stage for the political controversies and changes of the late nineteenth and early twentieth centuries. Nowhere were these conditions or changes more dramatic than in the nation's cities.

Between 1880 and 1920, of course, the American city came of age under the impact of industrialization; the dramatic new innovations in production, transportation, and communication; and the arrival of millions of foreign immigrants, mostly from eastern and southern Europe. The political challenges of the period were very much within this larger context.[16] By the beginning of the twentieth century, the American metropolis contained dozens of different ethnic and racial groups of many different nationalities, practicing a variety of religions. Electric streetcar lines radiated outward from the core, extending the city over a larger area and furthering the dual processes of spatial dispersal and social differentiation. The urban "community" had, in fact, become a number of different communities, or subcommunities, each with its own characteristics, territory, and even leadership. It was in this milieu that the urban political machine thrived: meeting the immediate needs of the lower classes on the one hand, and business on the other; balancing the interests of different communities and wards in city councils that were, admittedly, often inefficient and corrupt. But this complex and fragmented urban situation is critical to an understanding of urban politics and the nature of urban Progressive reform.

Mowry had certainly recognized the diversity of the "Progressives" and the presence among them of some very wealthy people. But the diversity of priorities and concerns among those who sought political change turned out, with further investigation, to be even more marked than the differences in their origins or socio-economic status. Some focused their fire on the industrial corporation and the "malefactors of great wealth"; others concentrated on controlling newly arrived immigrants, saving taxpayers' money, or shaping government in the image of Big Business efficiency.

Who the reformers were and what they wanted became increasingly complex issues as scholars examined their political conflicts with the urban political machines, and as the machines themselves were reexamined. The notion that urban political bosses were venal manipulators of the public will and corrupt parasites on the body politic—as was typically charged in contemporary reform rhetoric, and was picked up subsequently by Mowry and others—was challenged by a number of historians who looked at the actual functioning of the urban political machine, especially in the late nineteenth century, and assessed the boss's role in light of the interests and desires of his constituents.

The revised view of the urban boss emphasized the confusion and inefficiency of municipal governments in responding to the vast changes of the late nineteenth century, especially the impact of industrialization, an increase in urban scale and complexity, and the influx of millions of new city dwellers from different nations and cultures. New political organizations emerged to fill the vacuum, and they were dedicated primarily to seeking and maintaining political power and influence. The chief means for their success was, in most instances, majority support at the polls. Occasionally in some cities and often in others, illegal devices, strong-arm tactics, and bribery were essential tools of the urban political machine. But a good deal of the strength of the city boss was due simply to the fact that he and his organization enjoyed the support and confidence of the voters, and this support was generated, not so much from fear or stupidity or indifference, as from the realization that the boss was genuinely responsive to the desires and needs of the lower classes. As David P. Thelen observed of these newer interpretations, "We have come close to simply inverting the prejudices of the Progressive era."[17]

The machines were not, of course, altruistic, tolerant, or devoted to some developed notion of cultural pluralism and political equality; rather, they cultivated votes, in a methodical manner, in order to retain office and influence. Thus, bosses were often in the forefront of efforts to maintain low streetcar fares, provide minimal recreational spaces in lower-class communities, overlook the Sunday closing laws and other proscriptions against alcohol and other forms of "vice," and locate jobs for ordinary citizens. They were also not reluctant to use the powers of office—the police, building inspectors, and franchises for city services—to reward their supporters and punish their opponents. Other writers pointed to the fact that the reformers of the era who were able to address working-class and immigrant concerns and maintain political power for relatively long periods usually accomplished these goals through political organizations that functioned very much along the lines of the political "machine." John D. Buenker, especially, criticized Mowry and Hofstadter for ignoring the role of "new-stock" lawmakers and leaders in fashioning and forwarding reform in the nation's cities.[18]

These new views of the urban boss accompanied a reexamination of the role of urban reformers, and this investigation raised a number of questions about reformers' goals, methods, and motives. Kolko, Weinstein, and Hays suggested, of course, that "reform" was controlled mainly by the upper class and by corporate interests. A number of other writers of more traditional persuasion began to ask whether the "silk stocking" reformers wanted most to eliminate corruption and restore democracy to the cities or rather to cleanse the city and its immigrant and working-class masses of bad habits, insubordinate behavior, and moral imperfections. Some seekers after political change clearly concentrated on "purifying" the urban masses from a strongly nativist and middle-class perspective. On the other hand, there were those who battled the downtown business interests, fought for the municipal ownership of utilities, sought jobs for the unemployed and social services for their families, and largely ignored petty vices and the hours of saloons.

One explanation to clarify this apparent diversity was offered by Melvin G. Holli in his book, *Reform in Detroit*.[19] Apart from pointing out that Detroit mayor Hazen Pingree was both a reformer and the leader of an effective political "machine," Holli introduced a distinction between what he termed "social" and "structural" reform. The social reformers, by his definition, most closely fit the mold of the traditional view of the Progressives. Committed to the control of Big Business abuses and the provision of more adequate public services for the urban masses, leaders like Pingree,

Samuel "Golden Rule" Jones of Toledo, and Tom Johnson of Cleveland, fought municipal corruption while refusing to prescribe standards of morality for urban ethnic and religious groups. The structural reformers, on the other hand, placed their faith in "rule by educated, upper-class Americans and, later, by municipal experts rather than the lower classes."[20] William F. Havemeyer and John Purroy Mitchel of New York, Seth Low of Brooklyn, Grover Cleveland of Buffalo, and a number of academicians looked to the business corporation for models of city government, and sought economy, efficiency, and middle- and upper-class morality and standards of behavior as the bulwarks of what they deemed clean and decent cities. The structural reformers, according to Holli, were also concerned about limiting the influence of immigrants and other "uneducated" citizens in the political process, and they saw the masses of newly arrived immigrants and untutored voters as the foundation upon which the corrupt city politicians thrived. As James Weinstein observed, the prevalence of city-commission and city-manager forms of municipal government indicated the strength of the structural-reform tradition, where government was made especially responsive to the needs and demands of middle- and upper-class groups and major economic interests.

The problem with Holli's idea is that reformers simply did not divide neatly into such clear-cut groups. Activists like Jane Addams clearly met the criteria for "social" reformers, but they often also battled the big-city political machine and sought efficient and economical government. Conversely, many of those who wished to control and "improve" the behavior and morals of the lower classes also often promoted expanded social services. Paul U. Kellogg, for example, director of the 1907 Pittsburgh Survey, approached urban social problems with a sincere commitment to relieving the plight of the poor, but also with a typically elitist belief in the efficacy of trained social workers, the power of rationality, and the dangers of socialism and class violence.[21] Holli's distinction is important, however, in that it demonstrates the diversity (though not a chasm) among reformers, and it is a view that other scholars have found reasonably persuasive. Robert H. Wiebe, for example, noted that while "well-to-do merchants, manufacturers, and bankers who sought more dependable and rewarding relations with government were moving in the vanguard of reform," others, like settlement-house workers and other "humanitarians," were also "dreaming of an urban world that they would control for the benefit of all, a paradise of new-middle-class rationality." Wiebe also saw urban progressives increasingly taking two separate paths after 1905. "While one group used the language of the budget, boosterism, and social control, the other talked of economic justice, human opportunities, and rehabilitated democracy. Efficiency-as-economy diverged further and further from efficiency-as-social-service."[22] These two paths stemmed, according to Wiebe, from the desire of a new, and largely urban, middle class to find order, stability, and rationality in the chaotic reality of American cities. Reformers and corporations alike moved increasingly toward administration and bureaucracy as solutions to their problems.

The significance of the local business elite in political activities and changes was obviously slighted in the earlier literature. Rather than staunchly resisting alterations in government and public policy, urban commercial and professional leaders were crucial to their advocacy and adoption. Gabriel Kolko pointed, of course, to the highly conservative tendencies in progressivism, though his case was overstated. Samuel P. Hays concluded that the reforms advocated largely by the urban upper class—especially the forms of government and the methods of political participation—actually diluted democracy by limiting the participation of lower-class groups. The at-large system of voting, for example, effectively nullified the interests of minorities who were concentrated in specific neighborhoods or wards. The Progressive reform effort in the cities, in Hays's view, led to a centralization of government in the hands of the business elite, even though the rhetoric that accompanied such changes usually promised more widespread political participation than before.[23]

James Weinstein looked specifically at the widely heralded Progressive efforts to establish city-manager and city-commission forms of municipal government.[24] In contrast to the idea that the new governmental forms were implemented in response to lower-or middle-class demands, Weinstein argued that the "initiative for commission and manager government came consistently from chambers of commerce and other organized business groups; they were the decisive element, in coalition with civic reformers, which made the movement a sweeping success."[25] Modeled after the business corporation, the commission and manager forms were devised to insure economy as well as service, but elite control more than full-fledged participatory democracy. "The result of the movements," Weinstein claimed, "was to place city government firmly in the hands of the business class."[26]

Kolko, Weinstein, and Hays failed to provide a very precise definition of the "upper" class and how these upper-ranking groups could be distinguished from the "middle" class. But there is no longer any question that upper-ranking economic interest groups were extremely important in initiating political changes at the local level, and that most, if not all, of these changes were calculated to secure more firmly elite influence over public policy and even the political process itself. If anything, this was even more true in medium-sized communities than it was in the largest cities.

Much of the early twentieth-century reform impulse was a strain of nineteenth-century mugwumpery that emphasized elite education and the exercise of power by trained professionals and those with allegiances to "higher" principles and values: sobriety, hard work, social deference, regular routine, and abstract concepts of disinterested public service. Reform efforts often took on the coloration of religious benevolence and cultural philanthropy, with the "best" people striving to save the masses from sloth, degradation, and violence, and—not coincidentally—to enforce the mandates of middle-class, native-American morality and stifle the rise of socialism and other brands of radicalism and dangerous discontent.[27] Men of character and skill should, in that view, guide public affairs and set the model for public service and private behavior. Certain ideas extended from this orientation: civil service, "nonpartisan" local government, the suppression of vice and liquor, and the promotion of the "public interest." The public interest was defined by these middle- and upper-class reformers as the good of the "community as a whole" rather than as the advantage of the bosses or the narrow and parochial concerns of wards, neighborhoods, or particular groups. Needless to say, the good of the city as a whole was defined in largely traditional and middle-class terms. This was, in part, a response to the increasing cultural heterogeneity of the metropolis.

Even the structural reformers, in Holli's phrase, were interested in this larger public good, and they sought new organizations and administration as a means of generating more efficient public services for all—though on their own terms and according to their own priorities. Civil service was one of their major interests, and was the preeminent method of eliminating patronage and of bringing expertise and disinterestedness to local government. As a result of their efforts, as Martin J. Schiesl has commented, "these reformed bureaucracies... constituted the new power centers in urban affairs and were more entrenched than the bases of power of the political machine," certainly by 1920.[28]

One reflection—indeed, almost an archetype—of this approach to urban public policymaking was Robert Moses of New York, who entered government service from Yale University as a committed, idealistic advocate of efficiency, economy, skilled administration, and selfless public service. Like most other upper-class reformers, Moses had little sympathy for the parochial concerns of neighborhoods or the petty manipulations and corruption of the bosses. But, ironically, he came close to outdistancing Tammany in the development and consolidation of political power. Failing in his one effort in electoral politics, Moses became a notable force behind the scenes, especially in Albany. Through uncommon skill in drafting legislation, he was able to fashion powerful regional authorities (the Triborough Bridge Authority among them), of which he became the virtually impregnable master, removed from direct accountability to the electorate and insulated from other political attacks by the nature of his position and his influence through giant construction projects (and the lucrative contracts that went with them) and by clever political infighting. Standing almost aloof from politics, Moses was the "supreme bureaucrat." While he was clearly an exceptional figure, his career exemplified some of the inherent tendencies in the reforms advocated in the early twentieth century by middle- and upper-class groups.[29]

An understanding of urban politics in this period requires, of course, an appreciation of the process of urbanization and the specific social, economic, and spatial changes in American cities. As Samuel P. Hays observed, urbanization was characterized by a constant tension between centrifugal and centripetal tendencies— the "push" of outward population movement and the "pull" of increasing economic concentration. Economic growth and social mobility in the late nineteenth century created intense demands for social differentiation, for the creation of new subcommunities. "The desire for social differentiation," Hays wrote, "could be realized only through geographical differentiation."[30] This sorting out and fragmentation of social groups gave rise to a generally decentralized political system in the late nineteenth century, in which the ward was the fundamental political unit.

This political pattern, in turn, gave the lower classes and the ethnic and national minorities a voice—and sometimes a strong voice—in the councils of local government, and more often than not, this structure enhanced the influence of urban political machines that were firmly embedded at the ward level. As cities became larger and more differentiated, political controversies tended to become clashes among different areas of the city.

At the same time, improvements in technology—especially "organizational technologies" such as communications and new managerial techniques—led to the centralization of many urban functions and activities. Industrial capitalism brought forth the large corporation, which was itself a highly centralized economic and decision-making force. In place of the heterogeneous downtown area "came new activities which emphasized the central city as the location of organization which reached out to gather in the entire urban area. The large office building," Hays noted, "was the most dramatic physical expression of this change,"[31] just as U.S. Steel and Standard Oil were the most dramatic expressions of concentrated economic power.

Businessmen from larger companies—especially as they were organized in chambers of commerce—and rising professional groups encouraged these integrative tendencies in the early twentieth century. "The occupations of the upper class were often in the central city, the corporate systems in which it worked were headquartered there, and the property it owned often was either there physically or represented by investments in corporations based there. The urban upper class faced two ways at once; decentralist in residential institution, it was integrative in its economic and occupational life." Taken together, the integrative tendencies resulted "in a drive for integration and centralization in decision-making."[32] One of the first political attacks, then, was on the ward-based system of representation and other decentralized administrative arrangements for public schools and services. Later in the century, of course, this tendency toward centralization of municipal activities over a wider territory would reach a certain apogee in the regional authority for transportation, ports, water supplies, or recreation, of which Moses's organizations were exemplary. Ironically, however, the subcommunities created by the upper and middle social classes—the newer suburbs established beyond the municipal boundaries of the central city—grew more autonomous, while subcommunities within the central city became less and less important in the formulation of public policy.[33]

As annexations of growing settlements on the urban periphery grew increasingly difficult after 1910, some reformers called for consolidated urban governments in order to serve better their conception of the public interest. Even more common were efforts by upper-class leaders to establish federated systems whereby all communities would retain their identity but would be represented on area-wide governmental councils. In order to achieve efficient centralized administration without its attendant threats (largely social and economic) to their own subcommunities, they sought, as Jon C. Teaford observed, "to integrate the segregated metropolis through federation, not to mongrelize American life through the miscegenation of consolidated rule."[34] Zane L. Miller had discovered in Cincinnati a political division between the center and the periphery, with upper-class leaders often advocating, from their residential position on the urban fringe, a number of solutions to city problems, including home rule, strong mayoral systems of government, and at-large voting for city officials.[35]

By the 1920s, the turn-of-the-century fascination with the neighborhood, and the notion of the city as a collection of distinct parts, had given way to the city-wide, and even metropolitan area-wide, definition of political needs and problems. The "public interest" was defined in broader and broader geographical terms. This was, in part, a rational response to reality: cities were no longer tightly knit, congested places limited in scope by inefficient transportation systems. But it was also the result of efforts to bring larger, more complex, and more spread-out cities under the order and control of dominant social and economic groups and institutions.

The 1920s witnessed a continuation, even an intensification, of the quest for efficiency and social control, while the cries for economic justice and political democracy faded. The Depression of the 1930s forced an even broader perception of the public interest, an expanded role of government at all levels, and an end—at least for a time—to the movements for municipal home rule. But the New

Deal reemphasized the importance of administration, bureaucracy, planning, and the management of cities through technology and higher levels of expertise.[36]

There will doubtless never be universal agreement on the precise meaning of "progressivism" and whether or not it was a distinct "movement" or a vague collection of impulses for political change. It was certainly not, by almost any definition, a homogeneous phenomenon. As Mowry concluded, and Filene reaffirmed, it cut across geographical, socioeconomic, and formal political boundaries, and proceeded in "moral, political, economic, and intellectual" channels. It involved a number of people from the middle- and upper-ranking echelons, especially in the nation's cities, where municipal reform efforts helped set the stage for efforts and organizations at the national level.

Most of the disagreement over Mowry's view of progressivism has centered around his contention that progressivism made major changes in the economy and proceeded out of a desire to redistribute wealth and secure a greater measure of political democracy, and his belief that the "typical" Progressive leader was old-stock, middle-class, a businessman or professional, young, and well educated. That many reformers sincerely desired to open the political process to all citizens, improve the accountability of elected officials and bureaucrats to the public, and restrain the power of the giant corporation cannot be questioned. Kolko and Weinstein, especially, gave far less credit to these motives and impulses than can be justified. But we now know, also, that these purposes were sometimes more the stuff of rhetoric than action; at worst, they shrouded underlying attempts to carve out more security for corporations, upper-class groups, and professionals, sometimes at the expense of genuine mass political participation. On the whole, it does appear that in the early twentieth century, and later during the New Deal, corporate capitalism was shaped and adjusted to new circumstances, with the result that economic and political power in many ways gravitated to fewer and fewer hands. But this should not suggest that reforms were always calculated to buttress narrow economic interests or that they were always welcomed secretly by Big Business.

Mowry's definition of "typical" Progressive leaders does not sufficiently distinguish that group from others in the population, fully explain their motives and goals, or account for all the other groups that participated in urban or national reform during the early twentieth century. But this does not alter the fact that many reform leaders, especially in the cities, did indeed fit the description very closely. It would appear that Samuel P. Hays's "upper-class" leaders actually overlap significantly with Mowry's "middle-class" leaders. There is doubtless much more agreement on where many reform impulses originated than has usually been recognized. Mowry saw these leaders moving against the abuses of the corporations, whereas Hays, Kolko, and Weinstein concluded that they promoted the interests of the major economic entities. But, in either case, these were individuals of substance, background, and access to social and economic influence.

In the realm of urban politics and reform, we must start with the fact that cities in the early twentieth century—especially the big cities—were diverse and complex communities or, more accurately, collections of communities. Their complexity and diversity were both produced and accompanied by forces of industrialization, technology, and massive population movements. Politics and the political process adjusted to these social and economic realities and, for a wide variety of reasons, were inadequate to meet the needs of a rapidly changing metropolis. The demands upon government were virtually as diverse as the population itself. The lower classes desired jobs, housing, and assistance in survival and self-improvement. The middle class desired opportunity and communities that were clean, decent, and safe according to middle-class tastes and standards. The newer professional groups had even more ambitious aspirations: to mold their environments according to the highest dictates of expertise and service, and according to professional allegiances rather than to parochial local loyalties. The upper classes also sought to integrate the contending forces of the city in a corporate form, to order a new urban domain that stretched for miles in all directions and that represented unprecedented scope and economic power. The middle and upper classes sought to rationalize this new metropolis in a variety of ways, from providing succor to the lower classes to structuring government and institutions in such a way that the consequences of discontent would be minimized and policymaking would rest securely in the hands of trained and "responsible" individuals and groups. Put simply, progressivism and reform meant different things to different people, and it produced, not surprisingly, a variety of different coalitions on an array of issues in scores of communities across the country.

Those groups that held high social position and possessed economic resources tended to weigh most heavily in the political balance. And the gospels of efficiency, economy, and high standards of disinterested service to the public interest were paramount among middle- and upper-class reformers, even when they were joined by lower-class groups and leaders of more radical persuasion. If corporate power was controlled and directed in certain ways, if government became more active and involved, if new concepts of private property were generated—these changes usually had at least the partial support of wide segments of the middle and upper classes as well as, in many instances, working-class and immigrant groups, more radical reformers such as Ben Lindsey and Jane Addams, and even the old-line political machines like Tammany Hall.

Whatever the precise meaning of the term, the groups, individuals, and activities usually clustered under the rubric of "progressivism" remain immensely significant to the emergence of the United States as a modern state—industrial, corporate, and bureaucratic. And they are equally significant in the development of metropolitan America. As Robert Wiebe said, "Progressivism was the central force in a revolution that fundamentally altered the structure of politics and government early in the twentieth century."[37] Mowry could not have said it better.

NOTES

1. George E. Mowry, *The California Progressives* (Berkeley, Calif., 1951), p. v.

2. George E. Mowry, *Theodore Roosevelt and the Progressive Movement* (Madison, Wis., 1946), pp. 10-11.

3. Mowry, *California Progressives*, p. v.

4. Ibid., pp. 87-88. George E. Mowry, *The Era of Theodore Roosevelt and the Birth of Modern America, 1900-1912* (New York, 1958), especially chap. 5, "The Progressive Profile." Also see Aldred D. Chandler, Jr., "The Origins of Progressive Leadership," in *The Letters of Theodore Roosevelt*, 8 vols., ed. Elting E. Morison (Cambridge, 1954), 8:1462-65.

5. Mowry, *California Progressives*, p. 89.

6. Richard Hofstadter, *The Age of Reform: From Bryan to F.D.R.* (New York, 1955), pp. 131-72.

7. Gabriel Kolko, *The Triumph of Conservatism: A Reinterpretation of American History, 1900-1916* (New York, 1963), p. 2. Kolko defined conservatism as "the attempt to preserve existing power and social relationships."

8. James Weinstein, *The Corporate Ideal in the Liberal State: 1900-1918* (Boston, 1968), p. xv.

9. Samuel P. Hays, "The Politics of Reform in Municipal Government in the Progressive Era," *Pacific Northwest Quarterly* 55 (October 1964): 157-69. Among the studies cited by Hays as supporting evidence was William T. Kerr, Jr., "The Progressives of Washington, 1910-12," *Pacific Northwest Quarterly* 55 (January 1964): 16-27. Along these same lines, see Richard B. Sherman, "The Status Revolution and Massachusetts Progressive Leadership," *Political Science Quarterly* 78 (March 1963): 59-65, and Jack Tager, "Progressives, Conservatives, and the Theory of the Status Revolution," *Mid-America* 48 (July 1966): 162-75.

10. J. Joseph Huthmacher, "Urban Liberalism in the Age of Reform," *Mississippi Valley Historical Review* 49 (September 1962): 231-41, and John D. Buenker, *Urban Liberalism and Progressive Reform* (New York, 1973).

11. David P. Thelen, "Social Tensions and the Origins of Progressivism," *Journal of American History* 56 (September 1969): 232-41. Also see Thelen, "The Social and Political Origins of Wisconsin Progressivism, 1885-1900" (Ph.D. diss., University of Wisconsin, 1967), and Thelen, *Robert M. LaFollette and the Insurgent Spirit* (Boston, 1976).

12. Peter G. Filene, "An Obituary for 'The Progressive Movement,'" *American Quarterly* 22 (Spring 1970): 33.

13. John D. Buenker, John C. Burnham, and Robert M. Crunden, *Progressivism* (Cambridge, Mass., 1977), p. 74.

14. Robert H. Wiebe, *The Search for Order, 1877-1920* (New York, 1967), p. xiv.

15. Ibid., p. 166.

16. For an interesting and provocative study of the technological and economic factors that constrain and shape the political problems and policies of cities, see Alan D. Anderson, *The Origin and Resolution of an Urban Crisis: Baltimore, 1890-1930* (Baltimore, 1977).

17. David P. Thelen, "Urban Politics: Beyond Bosses and Reformers," *Reviews in American History* 7 (September 1979): 407.

18. See Lyle W. Dorsett, *The Pendergast Machine* (New York, 1968); Zane L. Miller, *Boss Cox's Cincinnati: Urban Politics in the Progressive Era* (New York, 1968); Seymour Mandelbaum, *Boss Tweed's New York*

(New York, 1965); and Jerome Mushkat, *Tammany: The Evolution of a Political Machine, 1789-1865* (Syracuse, N.Y., 1971). Two recommended collections on this subject are Alexander B. Callow, Jr., ed., *The City Boss in Perspective: An Interpretive Reader* (New York, 1976), and Blaine A. Brownell and Warren E. Stickle, eds., *Bosses and Reformers: Urban Poli-Politics in America, 1880-1920* (Boston, 1973). Excellent recent works are John M. Allswang, *Bosses, Machines, and Urban Voters: An American Symbiosis* (Port Washington, N.Y., 1977), and Michael H. Ebner and Eugene M. Tobin, eds., *The Age of Urban Reform: New Perspectives on the Progressive Era* (Port Washington, N.Y., 1977). For Buenker's views, see, especially, *Urban Liberalism and Progressive Reform.*

19. Melvin G. Holli, *Reform in Detroit: Hazen S. Pingree and Urban Politics* (New York, 1969).

20. Ibid., p. 163. For a sympathetic view of perhaps the ultimate "social" reform Progressive, see Charles E. Larsen, *The Good Fight: The Life and Times of Judge Ben B. Lindsey* (New York, 1972).

21. See Clarke A. Chambers, *Paul U. Kellogg and the Survey: Voices for Social Welfare and Social Justice* (Minneapolis, 1971).

22. Wiebe, *The Search for Order*, pp. 167-68, 170, 176.

23. Hays, "The Politics of Reform in Municipal Government," pp. 157-69.

24. James Weinstein, "Organized Business and the City Commission and Manager Movements," *Journal of Southern History* 21 (May 1962): 166-182. This article was reprinted in a slightly revised form and retitled "The Small Businessman as Big Businessman: The City Commission and Manager Movements," in Weinstein, *The Corporate Ideal in the Liberal State*, pp. 91-116. Quotations are taken from the latter version.

25. Ibid., p. 99.

26. Ibid., p. 115.

27. See John G. Sproat, *"The Best Men": Liberal Reformers in the Gilded Age* (New York, 1968); Paul Boyer, *Urban Masses and Moral Order in America, 1820-1920* (Cambridge, Mass., 1978); and Helen Lefkowitz Horowitz, *Culture & the City: Cultural Philanthropy in Chicago from the 1880s to 1917* (Lexington, Ky., 1976).

28. Martin J. Schiesl, *The Politics of Efficiency: Municipal Administration and Reform in America, 1880-1920* (Berkeley, Calif., 1977), p. 191. Also see Kenneth Fox, *Better City Government: Innovation in American Urban Politics, 1850-1937* (Philadelphia, 1977).

29. See Robert A. Caro, *The Power Broker: Robert Moses and the Fall of New York* (New York, 1974).

30. Samuel P. Hays, "The Changing Political Structure of the City in Industrial America," *Journal of Urban History* 1 (November 1974): 10.

31. Ibid., p. 17.

32. Ibid., pp. 21, 22.

33. See Thomas Lee Philpott, *The Slum and the Ghetto: Neighborhood Deterioration and Middle-Class Reform, Chicago, 1880-1930* (New York, 1978).

34. Jon C. Teaford, *City and Suburb: The Political Fragmentation of Metropolitan America, 1850-1970* (Baltimore, Md., 1979), p. 122.

35. See Miller, *Boss Cox's Cincinnati.*

36. See Blaine A. Brownell, *The Urban Ethos in the South, 1920-1930* (Baton Rouge, 1975), and Mark I. Gelfand, *A Nation of Cities: The Federal Government and Urban America, 1933-1965* (New York, 1975).

37. Wiebe, *The Search for Order*, p. 181.

2

AL SMITH AND THE NEW YORK STATE FACTORY INVESTIGATING COMMISSION, 1911-1915

David R. Colburn

For the 600 employees, mostly young Jewish women and Italian immigrant women, who worked at the Triangle Shirtwaist Company in the Asch Building on the corner of Washington Place and Greene Street, the week was nearly over. Another fifteen minutes and they would go home to spend Sunday relaxing, attending church, and enjoying the company of their families and friends. At approximately 4:30 P.M. on March 25, 1911, one worker on the eighth floor casually tossed a lighted cigarette on the floor, where it came in contact with a pile of cloth cuttings. The company prohibited smoking, but the rule was seldom enforced. A fire immediately erupted and spread rapidly through the highly flammable materials scattered about the floor. Several workers on the eighth floor and nearly everyone on the lower floors were able to escape from the intense heat and smoke by using the stairwell or the elevator. Many others on the eighth, ninth, and tenth floors were not aware of the danger; these workers continued sewing at their tables until the fire had engulfed most of the eighth floor.

Once the fire had been detected, workers experienced great difficulty in escaping from the work area because the doors had been locked to prevent employees and outsiders from stealing the garments. Those who managed to find their way into the hallway found themselves trapped by the fire. Several tried to escape down the stairwell but were turned back by the intense heat. Others, blinded by the smoke stumbled toward the elevator, only to find an empty shaft. They plunged quickly to their deaths. Many employees on the tenth floor escaped to the roof of the Asch Building, where they were assisted onto the adjoining roof of the New York University School of Law Building by the students.

For 143 employees, nearly all of whom were women, escape ultimately proved impossible. Most succumbed to the smoke. Two young girls were found with their arms clasped around each other's neck, their bodies badly disfigured by the fire. Several other women managed to break windows on the eighth, ninth, and tenth floors and escape momentarily to the ledge. A large crowd, many of whom had just left work, gathered on the street below to witness the rapidly unfolding drama. Police and firemen had also arrived on the scene, but the fire ladders extended only to the seventh floor, and their hoses only reached the eighth floor.

As the flames moved closer to the women on the narrow ledge, they began to jump, at first individually and then in groups. The firemen quickly deployed their nets, but the women had jumped from such extreme heights that they broke through the safety nets. The crowd began yelling at the women not to jump, but most preferred a quick death than a slow, torturous one at the hands of the fire. For what spectators felt was an eternity, the sky seemed to rain young, fragile bodies crashing with a sickening thud against the street or breaking through iron gratings on the sidewalks into the cellars of buildings. In the space of ten minutes, forty women plummeted to their deaths. One old policeman observed somberly: "It's the worst thing I ever saw."[1] Echoing his comments were the horror-struck onlookers and city and state officials—all demanding to know why so many died.

The fire had ended in minutes, but the memory of the event was to last for years, sparking a reform movement that would reshape New York politics and elevate to power two Tammany Hall stalwarts, Alfred E. Smith and Robert F. Wagner. Both men would have a great influence on state and national politics for the next two and a half decades. This essay examines Smith's role, in particular, in the investigation by the New York State Factory Investigating Commission of the Triangle fire, and the consequences it had for state politics and his political career.

In the aftermath of the Triangle Shirtwaist Company fire, officials revealed that the Asch Building complied with the fire standards set by the state. Alfred Ludwig, Acting Chief Inspector of the Building Department, declared that "the building in many respects was much better than the law required." Neither Max Blanck nor Isaac Harris, owners of the Triangle Shirtwaist Company, could be found criminally negligible for the conditions in their factory. The *New York Times* noted sardonically that "the walls are as good as ever; so are the floors; nothing is worse for the fire except the furniture and 141 of the 600 men and girls that were employed in its upper three stories." Smith, speaker of the state assembly, launched the demand for an investigation in Albany, declaring, "If the building in which the disaster happened complied with the building laws of this State, those laws should be revised at once."[2]

At this stage in his career, Smith was a relatively young (thirty-eight), hardworking politician, who was only slightly known outside the confines of the state legislature. He had attained this position of leadership by loyally adhering to the Tammany Hall line and supporting all measures and policies emanating from Hall headquarters on Fourteenth Street in New York City. Smith's legislative record was mediocre at best, and he had demonstrated little more than passing concern for the welfare of the common man prior to 1911.[3] Given his record and his political allegiance, why did Smith become a leader of the fire investigation and the factory-reform movement in New York?

In part, his role was shaped by the public protest in the wake of the fire. On March 26, the day after the fire, over 100,000 New Yorkers filed through the morgue to demonstrate their grief for those who died in the fire. An equal number gathered at the corner of Washington Place and Greene Street to view the remnants of the fire. On April 5, over 50,000 people lined the streets as the unidentified victims were taken to their graves. It was one of the largest outpourings of public grief in New York history.[4]

The Women's Trade Union League called a public meeting at the Metropolitan Opera House on the evening of the fifth to protest the conditions that had caused the Washington Place disaster. The crowd was so large that thousands were turned away by police and thousands of others stood outside the building to hear the speeches. Miss Rose Schneiderman, a fiery redhead who helped to lead a strike against the Triangle Shirtwaist Company in 1910, denounced the meeting as a lot of hot air and called for action. The blunt truth, she argued, was that the worker's life is cheap and property is sacred.[5]

Both wages and working conditions bordered on the scandalous in New York State. Men, women, and, in some cases, children worked six days a week and ten to twelve hourse a day for less than a living wage. Families frequently managed only by having the husband and wife and several children work. In its annual report, the U.S. Department of Commerce and Labor noted that working conditions reflected "the abundance of desirable labor available and the large immigrant population. . . ."[6]

Efforts to improve working conditions had grown out of the Progressive leadership that Governor Charles Evans Hughes provided New York from 1905 to 1909. Several of his labor proposals, however, were subsequently overturned by the state courts, which reflected the laissez-faire attitude of an earlier generation and the interest of the state's business leadership. Thus, for example, a 1907 law that banned night work for women and children was declared unconstitutional by the New York Court of Appeals because it violated the due process clause of the Constitution, which allowed employers and employees to negotiate freely over terms of employment.[7]

Working conditions in the garment industry were often worse than those in other factories. One of the largest garment manufacturers in New York City was the Triangle Shirtwaist Company. Owners Blanck and Harris followed typical practices in the industry: billing their female employees for needles and other supplies, charging them for clothing lockers, and imposing fines on them larger than the value of the goods they accidentally damaged. When several employees joined the International Ladies Garment Workers Union (ILGWU), Blanck and Harris fired them. Local 25 of the ILGWU then went on strike. The owners hired thugs to beat up the male strikers and prostitutes to mingle with the female workers in the picket line, impugning the reputation of the women. The strike was settled when Blanck and Harris agreed to rehire the union members and promised to improve working conditions. But, as Mary Dreier, president of the ILGWU, reflected, conditions did not improve. Instead, the owners fired the leaders of the strike, forced the experienced help to train Italian immigrant girls to sew skirts, and then fired all the experienced help who had gone on strike.[8]

Conditions faced by Triangle Shirtwaist employees were not exceptional. Many factories permitted working conditions that directly threatened the physical health of their employees. The demonstrations in the wake of the Triangle fire sought to awaken public interest, not only to the fire dangers in such factories, but also to the working conditions in these establishments.

A Committee of Safety, chaired by Henry L. Stimson, prominent New York Republican and Progressive, was organized to direct public pressure on state political leaders. This committee, together with the Women's Trade Union League, the National Consumer's League, and the ILGWU, maintained a steady clamor for remedial legislation.[9]

During the protests, Smith and Wagner had been quietly discussing proposals to investigate the fire and factory conditions with Governor John Dix and other legislative leaders. The two men sought support for a statewide investigation. Each seemed anxious to avoid having such an examination confined to New York City for fear that it would jeopardize Tammany Hall's political standing. In their discussions, they encountered very little opposition to a general investigation. Legislators seemed genuinely moved by the deaths from the fire as well as by the public demand for an investigation.[10]

At the end of June, a bill providing for a commission of nine members received approval by both houses. Smith was a strong advocate of the commission approach to investigating state problems. He felt that the legislature lacked the time to conduct such investigations because of its overriding concern with the state budget. He observed that during the Hughes era, the "very best kind of legislation" in gas insurance, fire insurance, and inferior court legislation had resulted from such commission studies.[11]

The commission included two members from the state senate, three from the assembly, and four appointed by Governor Dix. The members chosen to serve were Robert Wagner, Smith, and Charles M. Hamilton from the state senate; Cyrus W. Phillips and Edward D. Jackson from the assembly; Simon Brentano, of the New York publishing house; Robert E. Dowling, prominent real estate broker; Mary E. Dreier, social worker and activist; and Samuel Gompers, president of the American Federation of Labor (AFL). At the commission's organizational meeting on August 17, Wagner and Smith were named chairman and vice-chairman. The legislature directed the commission to fix responsibility for the loss of life in the fire and recommend legislation to protect workers in factories.[12]

A major problem immediately beset the commission. In an effort to curtail the scope of the investigation, conservative legislators had persuaded their colleagues to appropriate only $10,000 for the study. Smith noted that it would cost more than that to obtain a good legal counsel. He and Wagner talked to Henry Morgenthau, chairman of the Committee of Safety, about the commission's dilemma. "Are you folks going to finance this investigation?" Smith and Wagner asked. "Because, if you aren't, we don't see how it is to be carried on." Morgenthau told them that he knew an excellent lawyer who would serve as chief counsel for no fee—Abram I. Elkus of New York City. Morgenthau agreed to assist Elkus, also without charge.[13]

Throughout the course of what would become a four-year study, the commission received assistance from numerous industrial and labor experts. They included: Dr. George Price, former industrialist and expert on industrial safety, who headed the investigation of industrial sanitation; Dr. Howard B. Woolston, assistant professor of political science at the City University of New York and former social worker, who supervised the examination of wages; Dr. C. T. Graham-Rogers, a medical inspector of factories for the state Labor Department, who headed the study of lead works and lead poisoning; and H. F. P. Porter, expert on fire problems, who directed the study of fire safety and protection. Several women who had been involved in settlement work and in the ILGWU also participated in the investigation. These women had firsthand knowledge of factory conditions and their impact on the health and welfare of workers. Frances Perkins was secretary of the commission, while Belle Israels, Pauline Goldmark, and Josephine Goldmark all served as field investigators; Florence Kelley, General Secretary of the National Consumer's League, testified as one of many expert witnesses.[14]

Because of their familiarity with the working-class experience, these professionals sought to direct the commission's attention to the hazardous working conditions faced by workers. Frances Perkins wrote:

> We used to make it our business to take Al Smith . . . to see the women, thousands of them, coming off the ten-hour nightshift on the rope walks in Auburn [New York]. We made sure Robert Wagner personally crawled through the tiny hole in the wall that gave exit to a step ladder covered with ice and ending twelve feet from the ground, which was euphemistically labeled "Fire Escape" in many factories. We saw to it that the austere legislative members of the Commission saw with

their own eyes the little children, not adolescents, but five-, six-, and seven-year-olds, snipping and shelling peas.[15]

At first suspicious of Wagner and Smith because of their affiliation with Tammany Hall, these women soon became impressed by their efficient handling of the investigation and their commitment to remedy past abuses. What Perkins and her associates failed to realize was that Smith and Wagner were very sympathetic to the plight of workers. Their friends, neighbors, and relatives came from New York's Lower East Side and were predominantly lower-class, immigrant, blue-collar workers. What Smith and Wagner lacked was a knowledge of factory conditions. Neither had ever worked in a factory, and their knowledge came largely from conversations with family, friends, and constituents. Few, however, complained about working conditions, wages, or hours worked; most were just happy to have a job. Furthermore, few of Smith's or Wagner's constituents were likely to complain about factory conditions to them since Tammany's legislative delegation had not been advocates of labor reform prior to the Triangle fire. In reflecting on the developments of that year, Smith observed, "It was during the course of the investigations made by this commission that I got my first good look at the state of New York." In the process, Smith personally viewed factory conditions for the first time.[16]

Because of the dedication and unselfishness of these professionals, Smith and Wagner gradually changed their opinion of reformers as well. They were quite different from the New York Progressives on whom Smith and Wagner had based their earlier impressions: Smith and his Tammany associates had viewed New York's Progressives as a group of opportunistic "do-gooders." During past political campaigns, Progressives solicited votes in the immigrant sections of New York by denouncing "the corrupt Tammany Hall." Yet, once elected to office, these same Progressives paid little attention to the needs of voters. Instead, they reduced the budget, lowered taxes, and eliminated numerous jobs that had been held by recent immigrants. Neither Smith nor Wagner seemed surprised to find, during the course of the factory investigation, that an Auburn factory owned by Thomas Mott Osborne, a leader of Progressive Democrats in New York, had "the vilest and most uncivilized conditions of labor in the state."[17]

The commission began its formal hearings on October 14. Fourteen public hearings were held in New York City, and eight were scheduled for Buffalo, Rochester, Syracuse, Utica, Schenectady, and Troy. The committee experts and factory investigators screened witnesses and reported factory conditions to the commission. Smith encouraged investigators, not only to check for illegal violations in factory conditions, but also to comment on aspects that violated no law but that endangered the physical health of workers. Smith told inspectors that these reports would enable legislators to draft laws that would adequately reflect the needs of laborers.[18]

During its first year of operation, the commission concentrated principally on fire safety. Commissioners soon realized, however, that many more workers were injured or killed from dangerous working conditions than died from factory fires. As a result, commissioners decided to expand the scope of their investigation to include industrial accidents, diseases, wages, condition of employment of men, women, and children, and the homework, or sweating, system. As one member of the commission observed: "What is the use of demanding safe and sanitary factories, if the men who work in them cannot earn enough to support their families in health and comfort?" "In brief," Smith reflected, "it was the aim of the commission to devote itself to a consideration of the measures that had for their purpose the conservation of human life."[19]

In their examination of fire safety, commissioners learned that few owners violated state fire-code regulations. What they discovered, however, was that the laws were often inadequate to protect the workers. Testimony from a number of experts revealed that fireproofing a building kept the building from being destroyed in a fire, as was the case in the Triangle fire, but did not necessarily protect the workers' lives. H. F. P. Porter, who headed the investigation of fire safety, told commissioners that when he served as vice-president of the Vernet Lamp Company in Pittsburgh, he had pursued several nonexpensive steps such as more frequent fire drills and installation of additional fire escapes to insure greater protection for workers. Porter's personal experience as a businessman greatly influenced commissioners who were reluctant to mandate changes that would be expensive for owners to implement.[20]

The evidence gathered by investigators revealed that fires not only cost lives but that they also cost American businesses a great deal of money. According to a 1907 report, United States businessmen paid $215,084,709 in damages, or $2.51 per person, as compared with only thirty-three cents per person in Europe, where urban congestion was considerably greater and thus the potential damage from a fire much greater. Fire chiefs urged commissioners to require fire walls in all new buildings, noting that tests had shown them to be very effective in protecting life and property. They also recommended the use of sprinkler systems in all factories above eight floors since water hoses could not reach beyond the eighth story.[21]

While inadequate fire protection caused some concern among commissioners, and had been the issue that led to the investigation, their attention, during the first year of the investigation, quickly focused on working conditions. Investigators reported numerous incidents where health hazards had been ignored despite warnings from state field inspectors. Indeed, health hazards appeared to be an integral part of many factory jobs. In the hat industry, for example, investigators reported numerous cases of employees retiring at an early age because of diminishing eyesight caused by the use of wood alcohol in the stiffening process. All hat manufacturers who appeared before the commission admitted knowing that wood alcohol had damaged the eyesight and physically weakened many of their workers. They continued to use wood alcohol, however, because it was cheaper than the safer grain alcohol.[22]

Perhaps no conditions were more hazardous than those found in paint factories, where workers repeatedly succumbed to lead colic, which caused prolonged illness or, in some cases, death. By being constantly exposed to the lead fumes from the molten process in paint factories, workers suffered a change in skin color, constipation, spasmodic abdominal cramps, coated tongue, blue line on the gums, severe headaches, dramatic loss of weight, and, eventually, death. Lead poisoning did not discriminate against any particular ethnic or racial group. Investigators reported that Germans, Italians, Poles, Jews, Negroes, English, Scots, Hungarians, and Lithuanians had all experienced severe lead poisoning. One Italian immigrant who had worked in a lead factory lost from two to four days of work every month because of lead colic. Finally, he returned to Europe, declaring to friends that America had been "no good" for him.[23]

A typical case presented to the commission involved Stanley Irvine, thirty-six, an employee at the Splitdorf Magneto Company in New York City, who was forced to give up his job as a steel hardener because of severe lead poisoning. Irvine earned a respectable income of $15 a week, but several bouts with lead colic had caused him to lose sixty-one pounds and several weeks of work, for which he had not been compensated. The loss of work had pushed Irvine's family close to the poverty line. Irvine had been promised other work at the Splitdorf plant but had not received another position at the time he appeared before the Factory Investigating Commission. Clarence Shipman, a foreman at Splitdorf, tried to undermine Irvine's credibility by claiming that lead poisoning only affected those at the plant who drank heavily. But investigators found little evidence at Splitdorf or any other factory to support Shipman's contention.[24]

Investigators told commissioners that the United States was well behind Europe in protecting workers from lead poisoning. England, France, and Germany had all adopted laws requiring proper ventilation, forbidding food, beverage, and tobacco in the work area, and ordering factories to be cleaned at regular intervals. In England, workers were also required to take warm baths regularly, and records were kept by company officials.[25]

Commissioners heard numerous stories of conditions that were equally severe, if not as pervasive. Dr. Charles Graham-Rogers commented on the physical reaction that match workers had to phosphorous fumes, reporting on several cases in which phosphorus had been absorbed by the skin and decay of facial bones and the jaw had resulted. Similarly, acid fumes from soldering tinware at the Buffalo Forge Company had caused extensive internal damage to fifteen girls between the ages of sixteen and eighteen.[26]

As a resident of New York's Lower East Side, Smith readily sympathized with the plight of employees who faced such working conditions. His father had died at an early age from such hazardous conditions, leaving his mother alone to raise Al and his sister. The testimony of workers and investigators led Smith to assert that "the State is bound to do everything in its power to preserve the health of the workers who contribute so materially to its economic wealth and its industrial prosperity...."[27]

At the end of the commission's investigation in 1911, commissioners proposed several new laws to the state legislature. Smith and Wagner were given major responsibility to direct these proposals through the senate and the assembly in 1912. The key proposal was a bill to limit the working hours of women and children to fifty-four a week. This bill became the cornerstone of the New York Progressive effort. Commissioners argued that improvements in technology had placed great strain on women and the family in general, and that society could not afford to have the health of women and children impaired by hazardous working conditions and long hours. Citing a report on national vitality by Irving Fisher, the commission declared that "the point to be insisted upon is not that it is profitable for an employer to make the working day shorter . . . but to show that it is profitable for the nation and race."[28]

The commission also proposed a variety of bills designed to ease the loss of life in a fire. These included adequate fire exits, sprinkler systems, fire drills, and fireproofing. To protect workers more fully from health hazards, the commission proposed laws to provide separate eating facilities and adequate ventilation in factories using poisonous substances and generating large quantities of dust. The commission seemed especially interested in protecting women and children workers, requesting laws, in addition to the fifty-four-hour bill, preventing women from working after childbirth, providing seats for women in factories, and requiring physical examinations for children.[29]

The commission generally sought moderate, piecemeal reforms rather than comprehensive changes in factory conditions. The philosophy of the group seemed to be aimed at proceeding gradually to insure that their reforms did not place a severe economic hardship upon manufacturers, perhaps forcing them to close down and lay off their employees.

Under Smith and Wagner's direction, the factory legislation proceeded smoothly through the legislature. Opposition emerged chiefly to the fifty-four hour bill and the requirement for a sprinkler system in all factories above eight stories in height. The first proposal incurred the wrath of seasonal businesses and laissez-faire proponents in particular. The second was opposed chiefly because of its cost. Armed with testimony presented before the Factory Investigating Commission and field reports from investigators, Smith and Wagner persuaded their colleagues of the wisdom of the fifty-four-hour bill. It only passed the senate by two votes, however, and only after two senators who had left for home were recalled. The sprinkler-system proposal, however, was defeated. Significantly, the legislature endorsed Smith's proposal, extending the life of the commission for another year and providing it with general power to pursue its investigation of labor conditions throughout the state.[30]

During its second year, the commissioners continued their examination of the circumstances under which women and children worked. In particular, investigators looked into the homework, or sweating, system that allowed mothers to work while staying at home and supervising the children. The system appeared to be exceedingly beneficial to immigrant and lower-class families, where women as well as children had to work so that families could manage financially.

According to the Industrial Commission, the homeworker was generally a foreigner who had recently arrived in the United States, and was frequently a woman whose husband had died or was underemployed. The work was carried on in one or two rooms by the women and children. The family received its materials from special jobbers, or contractors, each a specialist in one line of clothing, who had been given cut and bunched materials for each garment from the manufacturer. With the distribution of the materials to the contractors, the manufacturer washed his hands of the business, remaining ignorant of how and where his finished goods were made.[31]

This method of employment had been nicknamed the "sweating system" because it paid very little and required long hours of work before a family would have anything to show for its labors. One women received one and one-half cents to two and one-half cents for each gross of buttons she carded. She averaged twenty-five gross per ten-hour day and never earned more than $4.50 a week. According to investigators, her health had been noticeably impaired under the strain of the homework system. One young girl told an investigator that because of the homework her mother performed, "I have no time for play, when I go home from school I help my mother."[32]

Al Smith's mother had supported her family by making umbrellas at home. Forced to work long hours to make a decent income to support her two children after the death of her husband, she turned to other work outside the home when her health was threatened. Recalling his mother's experience with the homework system, Smith felt that the state had a moral duty to "do everything it can for the preservation of the health of the child and women workers."[33]

The canning business, like the homework system, avoided state labor laws because it provided only seasonal work. Working conditions were typically harsh for women and children in this business. At one such factory, female employees carried pans and pails of tomatoes weighing twenty-five pounds each back and forth from the scalder to the checking station ten hours a day, six days a week, for very low wages. The industry employed large numbers of women and children to keep its labor costs low and its profit margin high. In commenting on the difficult physical labor endured by women in the canning business, one employer told an investigator that "it did women good to stand and carry pans and pails: 'It gives them exercise!'" Children also worked excessively long hours in canning factories. One twelve-year-old boy said that he worked from 4:30 A.M. to 10 P.M. during the height of the season. He went to bed at 11 P.M. and slept to 3:30 A.M., when his mother would awaken him. The child was very slender for his age, his face had little color, and his eyes had no spark of youth. Smith viewed the conditions encountered by women and children in the canning industry with great derision: "Many of the cannery-owners evidently held the theory that shelling peas and preparing fruit was a recreation."[34]

The employment of children under such conditions had a profound effect on the commissioners, who were especially moved by children who testified about their working experiences. Fifteen-year-old Josephine Kauffman told commissioners that she had been forced to leave school at the age of thirteen to help her parents support her three brothers and three sisters. She worked at a garment factory, clipping threads and buckling up pants. It took her from forty-five minutes to one hour to get to work, depending on how far she chose to walk to save taxi fare. She arrived at work before sunrise and returned home after sunset. Mary Carter, fourteen years old, worked at the Golden Globe Mills in Utica, where she averaged $5.00 a week for sixty hours of work. She and twenty-three other girls asked for a wage increase and were all fired by the manager. The boss also withheld three days' wages from their final check. Carter's hands were badly cut and bleeding from the piecework she had done at the factory.[35]

Commissioners attempted to determine how many children

under the age of fourteen were being employed by manufacturers, but this proved very difficult to do. Union members recounted stories of how children under fourteen were sent out to a park, given the day off, or hidden between floors to avoid meeting state factory inspectors.[36]

On the basis of this testimony and investigative reports, the commission proposed that the state Department of Labor be reorganized to give it ample power to enforce child-labor laws. The commission further recommended the prohibition of women and children in factories between 10 P.M. and 6 A.M., and the employment of children. It also banned children from operating dangerous machinery or from working in a trade that might be harmful to their health. Stricter tenement regulations were proposed to regulate the sweating industry and its exploitation of women and children in school; scholarships for the underprivileged were also recommended. Other major proposals included the creation of a five-member state Industrial Board to oversee working conditions in dangerous trades, a workmen's compensation law to protect the injured and ill, regulation of bakery conditions, prohibition of smoking in factories, and improved sanitation for workers, including washrooms and separate lockers in foundries.[37]

Support for the work of the commission had become so widespread among Progressive groups, working classes, and the press that the measures received the endorsement of the legislature, despite opposition from conservative business leaders and realtors. Governor William Sulzer approved all the bills except the proposed workmen's compensation program, which he regarded as too expensive for employers. The legislature, however, passed the measure over his veto in a special session. Samuel Gompers called the compensation act "the best of its kind ever passed in any state, or in any country." The New York Federation of Labor declared that "no Legislature in the history of the State Federation surpassed the session of 1913 in the passage of so many or so important remedial measures for wage earners of New York State...."[38]

Significantly, the state courts upheld the constitutionality of the new labor laws. The prohibition against women and children working between 10 P.M. and 6 A.M. had been adopted originally in 1899 but declared unconstitutional in 1907. The commission included in its proposal a sociological brief explaining the need for such legislation. In 1915, the New York Court of Appeals reversed its earlier ruling, citing new information gathered by the Factory Investigating Commission.[39]

The investigation revealed that women and children, in particular, were very poorly paid, and that most women could not afford an independent living on the wages they received. Women earned an average weekly income of $6.00. A typical weekly expense sheet for a woman making this income disclosed the following:

Half of a furnished room	$1.50
Breakfast and dinner	2.10
Lunch	.70
Carfare	.60
Clothes at $52/year	1.00
TOTAL	$5.90[40]

A six-dollar income did not permit a woman to rent her own apartment. It also left no room for medical or dental care, amusements, or a newspaper. The custom of "letting it [illness] go on" was one of the chief explanations for the anemic condition of so many working women. Since they could not afford to visit a doctor or a dentist, women usually waited until an illness became serious before they sought medical attention. If a woman worked an entire year at this rate, she could save $5.20. But if she was engaged in a seasonal occupation or became ill, her savings would disappear in one week.[41] One girl told the commission that she had not taken a vacation in six years because she could not afford to lose her salary for a week or two. "I feel sometimes I'm not really living—I'm just existing," she said.[42]

A department store clerk who earned $6 a week told commissioners, "When I have to pay for a pair of shoes or something like that, I don't buy meat for weeks at a time." Another clerk remarked that "I never eat any breakfast at all. By experience I found that was the easiest meal to do without."[43]

When asked why they worked for such trifling sums, the women usually replied: "To eat," "To help take care of my family," "To dress my children right," or "To save money to buy a home." The explanation, and frequently the excuse, for the prevalence of low wages paid to women was the assumption that they did not need to be self-supporting since they lived at home. However, the investigation showed that 62 percent of all women and girls employed were unmarried and self-supporting. Mindful of the need for women to work, the commission examined ways to protect their health and welfare. As vice-chairman Smith noted: "In the ordinary nature of things we might say that women have no place in industry, but we have to face actual conditions. Even the employment of children is sometimes necessary."[44]

The increased prostitution in New York was directly blamed on low wages. Katherine Davis, an investigator, reported that many women who turned to prostitution had a poor income with little hope of ever receiving a pay raise. Forced to subsist on such small sums, these women found prostitution a rather easy way to supplement their income. One woman who earned a mere $2.37 per week in a shoe factory lived with a bartender over a saloon because she could not afford her own place and adequately feed herself. He had encouraged her to work as a prostitute to provide them both with an additional income."[45]

Others who refused to engage in such activities often lived in "red-light" districts and endured the temptations of prostitution because they could not afford to live elsewhere. A young woman laconically told an investigator that her neighborhood was not a "red-light" district, but the "lights were getting pinker every year." The commission strongly criticized the evils that encouraged women to become prostitutes. "No words of ours can express too strongly our condemnation of the inhuman greed and avarice that permits women to be thus exploited."[46]

During discussions of minimum-wage legislation, manufacturers and labor unions joined forces to oppose such a wage. Employers alleged that while they were working toward "a maximum wage," they opposed state legislation because it would raise the cost of their products to consumers and cheapen the dollar. Unions feared that the minimum wage, if adopted, would quickly become the maximum wage. However, attorney Louis Brandeis, proponent of Oregon's minimum-wage law and a leading labor-reform spokesman, argued that such a wage would actually reduce expenses for manufacturers, after an initial period of introduction. "Not only is the employee worth more but the employer exerts himself to make the employee more efficient," Brandeis reported. He also noted that in Massachusetts, where a minimum-wage law had been adopted for women, manufacturing had prospered and higher wages had resulted. Smith questioned Brandeis closely about the constitutionality of a minimum wage in New York, in light of the conservative composition of the courts in the state. But Brandeis responded that he thought, if they followed the minimum-wage legislation established in Oregon and Massachusetts, there would be no constitutional questions.[47]

The commission proposed a minimum wage of $8.00 a week for women and children, arguing that they needed the protection of the state. The commissioners felt that men had the protection of labor unions, and consequently did not need assistance from the state on wages. Wagner proposed the creation of a Wage Commission to provide a minimum wage for women and children. Conservative legislators argued successfully, however, that such legislation was unconstitutional, and the measure was rejected.[48]

The evidence accumulated by the Factory Investigating Commission presented a sad commentary on industrial America in the twentieth century. Exploitation of women and children seemed to characterize most business operations in New York. The family and the physical health of its working members appeared to be seriously jeopardized by the pressures and hazards of industry, without so much as a second thought from most business leaders. The growth and consolidation of industry and the massive immigration during these early years of the twentieth century increased the impersonalization in the economic sector. The Factory Investigating Commission made the public aware of the magnitude of the problem and the difficulties it posed for workers, their families, and society. In order to insure protection for the worker and the family, the commission argued persuasively that it was essential for the state to intervene.

Aroused by the evidence presented during the investigation, the public demanded corrective legislation. The record distinctly reveals that the years 1911 through 1915 were peak years of Progressive legislation in New York, and, as J. Joseph Huthmacher has noted, "... it clearly indicates, too, that an essential element in the compilation of that record was Tammany Hall."[49]

Still under the shadow of Boss Tweed, and more recently Richard Croker, Tammany was in search of new programs to reawaken voter interest in the organization. Charles F. Murphy, the leader of Tammany since 1902, realized that granting reforms could be politically profitable, so long as these reforms did not undermine the power of the machine. He had seen former Governor Charles Evans Hughes, an avowed reformer, lead the Republican party to victory at the polls from 1905 to 1909. Having listened to the older politicians in Tammany, and having had little statewide political success, Murphy, in 1910, decided to change course and bring his organization under fresher winds. According to Al Smith, the new advisers included Congressman Thomas Smith, State Senator Robert Wagner, Assemblyman James Foley, and himself. Also, from time to time, individuals who had special knowledge of information on some piece of legislation were called in to advise Murphy.[50]

Because they were young men aspiring for greater political success, these new advisers remained attuned to public sentiment, unlike many of the elderly Tammany politicians who remained sequestered at the Hall. As one observer put it: "... while they [Al Smith, Wagner, Foley] weren't above reasonable protection of the interests of the organization, they weren't completely dominated by it either." They found Murphy a willing listener and a good adviser."[51]

Convinced of the Factory Investigating Commission's importance by his new advisers, Murphy supported it and the resulting reform legislation. Smith claimed that because Murphy "had come up from lowly surroundings, he took a keen interest in bills embodying social legislation." However, as Miss Perkins later noted, the legislation "was not only successful in effecting practical remedies but, surprisingly, it proved to be successful also in vote-getting."[52]

Despite the disillusioning effect of the investigation, Al Smith did not lose his faith in American capitalism. Often removed from a firsthand knowledge of daily operations, the owners were frequently ignorant of the conditions under which their employees worked. Once informed, Smith found them quite willing to make the needed improvements. "I have a world of confidence," Smith declared, "in the good sense and good judgment and desire for fair play of the manufacturers and business men of this state." Nevertheless, legislation was essential to establish standards. Smith was convinced that "such legislation was not only humanitarian ..., but was bound to promote efficiency, to increase productivity, to bring a spirit of harmony between capital and labor."[53]

As leaders in their respective chambers, Senator Robert Wagner and Assemblyman Al Smith were primarily responsible for much of the legislation drafted by the commission. Frances Perkins declared that "they became firm and unshakeable sponsors of political and social measures designed to overcome conditions unfavorable to human life."[54] By the close of their legislative careers in 1915, Smith and Wagner's names had been inscribed on most of New York's labor legislation. Smith's role on the Factory Investigating Commission introduced him to many of the pressing social and economic problems facing New York as it adjusted to the processes of industrialization and modernization in the early twentieth century. It also exposed him to a group of reformers and settlement workers whose knowledge of working-class problems would greatly assist him in addressing those concerns. He was able to combine the ideas of these reformers with the political wisdom and instincts he had developed as a Tammany Hall legislator to become New York's leading politician in the decade of the 1920s. The public visibility he attained while on the commission and the insights he acquired helped insure his election as governor of New York in 1918. His experience on the commission thus served as a major turning point in Smith's career, opening the door to higher political office and opening his eyes to the role the state could play in insuring a better society for all its citizens.

NOTES

1. *New York Times*, Mar. 26, 1911, pp. 1-3, and *Preliminary Report of the Factory Investigating Commission*, 3 vols. (Albany: J. B. Lyon Co., Printers, 1912), 1:35-38.

2. *New York Tribune*, Mar. 27, 1911, p. 1; *New York Times*, Mar. 26, 1911, p. 1; *New York Tribune*, Mar. 27, 1911, p. 5. Four more bodies were discovered after that report.

3. See Alfred E. Smith, *The Citizen and His Government* (New York: Harper, 1935); Smith, *Up to Now: An Autobiography* (New York: Viking Press, 1929); Beverley Robinson and James W. Wadsworth Reminiscences, Oral History Research Office, Columbia University, N.Y., for a look at Smith's early career in the state assembly.

4. *New York Times*, Apr. 6, 1911, p. 1.

5. Ibid., p. 10.

6. U.S., Department of Commerce and Labor, *Manufacturers, 1905*, 2 vols. (Washington, D.C.: Government Printing Office, 1907), 2:746.

7. Edward Robb Ellis, *The Epic of New York City* (New York: Coward-McCann, 1966), p. 489.

8. Colonel George B. McClellan, Jr., Family Papers, Subject File—P. W., Shirtwaist Makers Strike, Manuscript Division, Library of Congress; *New York Tribune*, Jan. 3, 1910, p. 3; and *New York Times*, Mar. 27, 1911, p. 3.

9. Smith, *Up to Now*, pp. 90-91.

10. *New York Herald-Tribune*, May 9, 1911, p. 2; and *New York Times*, July 1, 1911, p. 1.

11. *Preliminary Report of the FIC*, 2:12.

12. Smith, *Up to Now*, p. 92.

13. Henry Morgenthau, *All in a Life-Time* (Garden City, N.Y.: Doubleday, Page and Co., 1922), p. 108.

14. J. Joseph Huthmacher, *Senator Robert F. Wagner and the Rise of Urban Liberalism* (New York: Atheneum, 1968), pp. 5-6, and *New York Times*, Aug. 18, 1911, p. 5. Also see *Second Report of the FIC*, 4 vols. (Albany: J. B. Lyon Co., Printers, 1913), 1:13.

15. Frances Perkins, *The Roosevelt I Knew* (New York: Viking Press, 1946), p. 22.

16. Smith, *Up to Now*, p. 96.

17. Oscar Handlin, *Al Smith and His America* (Boston: Little, Brown, 1958), pp. 59-60.

18. *Preliminary Report of the FIC*, 1:23; ibid., 2:92.

19. *New York Tribune*, Mar. 27, 1911, p. 5, and Smith, *Up to Now*, p. 93.

20. *Preliminary Report of the FIC*, 1:145.

21. Ibid., 1:28, and ibid., 2:582-83, 1504-07.

22. *Second Report of the FIC*, 2:958-59, 998-1003.

23. *Preliminary Report of the FIC*, 1:446, and ibid., 3:1678.

24. Ibid., 3:1689-91, 1703-05.

25. Ibid., 1:373.

26. Ibid., 2:289, 787.

27. Norman Hapgood and Henry Moskowitz, *Up from the City Streets: A Biographical Study in Contemporary Politics* (New York: Harcourt, Brace and Co., 1927), p. 65.

28. *Preliminary Report of the FIC*, 1:28-111.

29. Ibid.

30. *New York Times*, Mar. 30, 1912, p. 2.

31. U.S., Congress, House, *Report of the Industrial Commission*, 15:324, 329, 369. Also in Oscar Handlin, *Immigration as a Factor in American History* (Englewood Cliffs, N.J.: Prentice-Hall, 1959), pp. 64-66.

32. *Second Report of the FIC*, 2:714, and ibid., 1:103.

33. Smith, *Up to Now*, p. 7, and Alfred E. Smith, "Labor Laws and Women Workers," *The Survey* 64 (May 15, 1930): 182.

34. *Second Report of the FIC*, 2:145.

35. *Preliminary Report of the FIC*, 3:1054-56.

36. Ibid., 3:1094.

37. *Second Report of the FIC*, 1:298-395.

38. *New York Times*, Apr. 5, 1913, p. 4; ibid., Dec. 14, 1913, p. 1; David M. Ellis et al., *A Short History of New York State* (Ithaca, N.Y.: Cornell University Press, 1957), p. 389.

39. *New York Times*, Mar. 27, 1915, p. 7, and Robert H. Bremer, *From the Depths: The Discovery of Poverty in the United States* (New York: New York University Press, 1956), pp. 237-38.

40. *Fourth Report of the FIC*, 1:36.

41. Ibid., 1:37. Men earned an average of $15 per week and children, $3.50. *Preliminary Report of the FIC*, 3:1984.

42. *Fourth Report of the FIC*, 1:37-38, and ibid., 4:1684.

43. Ibid., 4:1675.

44. *Second Report of the FIC*, 2:453; *Fourth Report of the FIC*, 1:37, 1494; and Smith, "Labor Laws and Women Workers," p. 182.

45. *Fourth Report of the FIC*, 1:36, and ibid., 4:1563.

46. Ibid., 4:1675, and *Second Report of the FIC*, 1:118.

47. *Fourth Report of the FIC*, 5:2710, 2882.

48. *New York Times*, Mar. 17, 1915, p. 6, and ibid., May 14, 1915, p. 9.

49. J. Joseph Huthmacher, "Charles E. Hughes and Charles F. Murphy: The Metamorphosis of Progressivism," *New York History* 46 (January 1965): 25.

50. Smith, *Up to Now*, p. 122.

51. Robert S. Binkerd Reminiscences, Oral History Research Office, Columbia University, N.Y., p. 59.

52. Perkins, *The Roosevelt I Knew*, p. 23.

53. Smith, "Labor Laws and Women Workers," p. 182, and "Smith as an Administrator," *Review of Reviews* 78. pp. 347-48.

54. Perkins, *The Roosevelt I Knew*, p. 17.

3

GINO C. SPERANZA: REFORM AND THE IMMIGRANT

George E. Pozzetta

The relationship between immigration and reform during the Progressive era has been the subject of considerable historical debate. Early studies examining the connection between immigrants and settlement houses and social-welfare programs, for example, tended to accept at face value the testimony of actual participants in these activities. Written from the perspective of middle-class, native philanthropists, these works normally stressed the theme of selfless humanitarianism at work to relieve human suffering and maladjustment.[1] Later reappraisals pointed out that other purposes were often at work in those endeavors. As one study observed, reform agendas also included a startling frequency of "indoctrinating or socializing children, Americanizing immigrants, serving up heavy doses of religion or morality, enforcing social order among the poor, and in general acting as instruments of social control."[2] Reinterpretations have admitted to some exceptions to that pattern —the International Institutes, for instance—but the full range of reform activities remains to be explored. There were many variations of strategies and motivations, and each can afford its own perspective on the complex reality of social change in America. A case in point centers on the career and personality of Gino Carlo Speranza.

As a successful lawyer in turn-of-the-century New York City and a proponent of immigration reform, Speranza attempted to deal with a myriad of problems besetting the massive numbers of Italian immigrants then flowing into America. During his multifaceted career, he spoke and wrote eloquently about the nature of this folk movement, seeking to achieve a degree of mutual understanding between immigrant and native. With equal vigor, he helped to organize and sustain a variety of organizations and campaigns that struggled to correct the abuses suffered by newcomers. Unlike many activists, Speranza was able to see immigration in its international context, and he worked effectively to enlist the support of agencies and individuals on both sides of the Atlantic. Until he left New York to work on the Italian front during World War I, he was one of the city's most articulate lobbyists for immigration reform and one of America's earliest proponents of cultural pluralism. Ironically, in the postwar years, he became an ardent supporter of 100-percent Americanism and total assimilation. The troubled path that led Speranza to this position helps shed light on the changes taking place in approaches to social reform, and tells us something about the nature of Italian immigration to America.

Speranza's early years were set, not in the steaming tenements of the Lower East Side, but rather in a comfortable, middle-class home in the suburbs of New York City. His father, Carlo Leonardo Speranza, was a university-educated specialist on Dante who had come from Verona in 1870 to teach at Yale University. When Gino was born on April 23, 1872, his father held a position as professor of Italian letters at Columbia University. The family returned frequently to Verona, however, and the young boy spent nine years of his youth there, during which time he received part of his early education. Consequently, he entered adolescence with a thorough grounding in both cultures and a fluency in English and in Italian. Gino carried these talents with him into a college program at the City College of New York, from which he was graduated in 1892. A law degree from New York University followed two years later, and by 1895, the young man was admitted to the bar and had already embarked upon a busy career.[3]

International law was Speranza's legal specialty; his particular interests resided in those matters that touched upon Italy and America, which inevitably involved him in the legal ramifications of Italian immigration to America. The great port city of New York was an especially appropriate location in which to develop these connections. The overwhelming bulk of Italian immigrants passed through New York on their way to other areas, and the city itself counted a foreign-born Italian population of 225,000 by 1900.

Speranza further broadened his contacts with this immigration flow in 1897 by accepting a position as legal consul to the Italian consulate general in New York.[4] In the next two decades, he intervened in the cases of hundreds of immigrants who encountered difficulties in the New World. Speranza was thus able to witness the legal and human implications of the Italian immigration process— from Italian village to American urban center to remote work camps—as did few other persons in America. Moreover, he came to possess a sensitivity to the inner fabric of the Italian immigrant community that largely eluded other social-welfare workers of the time.

Speranza first turned his energies to investigating the disadvantages that immigrants labored under when they encountered the American legal system. He found numerous instances in which Italians were denied due process or full protection of their rights. Speranza was especially critical of the boards of special inquiry at immigration stations that passed on cases involving aliens. These boards made thousands of judgments each year but, in his opinion, did so inadequately. Matters were routinely decided, not by judicial courts, but by "committees of government employees of a low hierarchical grade, laymen not lawyers, yet wielding a most tremendous power without other guarantees than their conscience."[5] Since the possibility of appeal was extremely limited, board decisions, which separated families, settled estates, and determined countless other critical matters, were usually final.

Problems of a different nature characterized the workings of courts in the city. Here, Speranza singled out interpreters as "the greatest handicap in the way of legal redress or protection" of Italians. In order to educate the great mass of citizens who never witnessed the daily operation of courts, he lectured extensively on the subject. One investigation of his described an interpreter system that was "insufficient in numbers, imperfect, ill-administered and in numerous instances carried into execution by ignorant and incompetent men."[6] Many municipal courts assigned detectives to interpreting work during sessions of police court, despite the obvious questions of propriety that practice raised. An exasperating problem further affecting Italians involved the multiplicity of often mutually unintelligible dialects used by immigrants. Newcomers frequently claimed that their cases were not being presented adequately or fairly, and that they did not understand rulings made by judges. Speranza lobbied persistently, albeit unsuccessfully, for a state bureau authorized to investigate and supervise all interpreters in the state and to examine the entire matter of boards of special inquiry.[7]

From his unique position, Speranza was able to investigate and report on the nature of the legal adjustments taking place within the immigrant community itself. He noted that among the millions of Italians coming to America were *avvocati* (lawyers) and law students. A large number of these individuals were unable to adjust to the American legal system and were forced into other trades or quasilegal professions. Some became agents, or "runners," for American lawyers; others became notaries. In fact, the names of recently arrived Italian immigrants soon occupied a conspicuous place on the lists of notaries in New York.[8]

In working out their new social order in America, practitioners drew upon the respect and position occupied by the *notai* (notaries) in Italy. In the Old World, the notary was a man of character, education, and standing in the community who had gone through a lengthy process of training and certification. The lax requirements for such a title in America, and the fundamentally different nature of the position, allowed many individuals to join the ranks. In short order, saloon keepers, boarding-house owners, and steamship agents by the hundreds proudly displayed the notary seal on their business windows. Many of these men subsisted on a variety of petty frauds that exploited the immigrants' incomplete understanding of the role played by notaries in America.[9]

Notaries frequently used the inevitable delays encountered in the American legal system to extract fees from immigrants in return for empty promises to expedite matters. They also often worked hand-in-glove with labor agents and bankers to fleece more hard-earned dollars from immigrant pockets by charging money for affixing unnecessary seals and stamps to documents. In Speranza's eyes, however, the "meanest fraud of all" was the collusion between such men and dishonest undertakers who worked to cheat immigrant families of their small estates. Undertakers and notaries filed bogus debtor's claims against estates, which often left survivors penniless. Similar practices abounded in the handling of injury assessments and in the transmission of settlement funds to Italy.[10] Legal redress for immigrants trapped in these situations was usually not available, and losses had to be absorbed.

By the turn of the century, Speranza and others who were attempting to better the lot of New York's Italian immigrants could look back at a record of dismal failure. A handful of efforts had been born—occasionally, with the backing of the Italian Government—but each had been quickly co-opted by the *prominenti* of the immigrant community. Composed primarily of bankers, labor agents, boarding-house owners, and the like, these individuals considered their own narrow interests threatened by reform activities. Consequently, they emasculated every attempt to change existing conditions and provide for effective regulation and policing of fraudulent activities. Instead, they expended their energies in bombastic rhetoric and emotional fund-raising campaigns designed to erect statues of famous Italian heroes.[11] Individual efforts to dramatize conditions, such as Speranza's writings and lecturings, were similarly ineffective in altering the entrenched position of the *prominenti*. What was needed now, in the view of many, was a formal organization, funded and directed from outside the ethnic community by persons owing allegiance to none of the internal community powers.

Speranza saw just such an opportunity in 1901, when the Society for the Protection of Italian Immigrants began operations. He hoped that the society and its varied programs would be able to establish a protective web around immigrants from the moment they left the homeland until they were safely in the hands of family or friends in America. The society began as a result of the efforts of Miss Sara Wool Moore, a New York City settlement-house worker, who took it upon herself to bring together a group of reform-minded individuals. An organizational meeting held on February 5, 1901, resulted in the dissemination of a promotional flyer, and, on March 18, in the acquisition of formal incorporation papers. The new society's charter proclaimed its intention to "afford advice, information and protection of all kinds to Italian immigrants, and generally to promote their welfare. . . ."[12] Given the range of problems then besetting Italian immigrants, this was a formidable task.

As the only active member of the executive board who was Italian, Speranza occupied a central role in the initial formation and direction of the society. With his knowledge of the immigrant community, he attempted to steer the society into channels that offered the greatest prospect of success. He believed it essential that the organization be strictly nonsectarian.[13] Speranza knew that much potential support among immigrants would be lost by having any religious affiliation (or even the perception of such ties). Indeed, despite his best efforts, the society was unable to avoid identifications of that sort. Before the end of the first year, a number of priests circulated statements claiming that the society was a Protestant organization seeking to convert immigrants from their "idolatrous beliefs."[14] Speranza also insisted that the society be operated as an American organization working for the betterment of immigrant conditions, not as a creature of the Italian Government. From his work with the Italian consulate, he knew well the depths of antigovernment sentiment among immigrants, and the disastrous effects this animus had had on previous reform attempts.[15] Subsequent events demonstrated the wisdom of his advice.

Money was the next objective of the fledgling organization, and Speranza, again, proved to be instrumental in finding solutions. As corresponding secretary, he wrote to numerous philanthropists to solicit money for society programs. A source of dependable, regular income was needed, however, and for this, Speranza quietly went to the Italian Government. By early 1902, he had ratified an agreement with Luigi Bodio, director general of the Italian Department of Emigration. The Italian Government pledged an annual, unrestricted subsidy of some $7,000 (later increased to $10,000), which provided a foundation from which to begin work. Equally important, the society received free office space and clerical help in a building owned by the Italian consulate at 17 State Street.[16]

From this base of operations, the society began its program of services to the immigrants. The directors mandated as the first priority an effort to strike at the thousands of runners, express men, and "steerers" who lurked near the Battery Landing area and Grand Central Station to entrap newly arrived immigrants with a variety of subterfuges. These men were usually agents for unscrupulous boarding-house keepers, saloon owners, labor agents, and confidence men. They perpetrated an endless variety of swindles and were controlled only by the limits of their own imaginations. Speaking familiar languages and promising needed services, these men routinely bilked newcomers of their carefully accumulated cash reserves.[17]

The society established a corps of uniformed guards and watchers, who took charge of immigrants as they exited from Ellis Island and the train stations. Ordinarily, society staffers gave immigrants an identification tag and brought them to the Battery Landing, where other personnel took charge until the travelers were deposited at society offices. These services aroused the opposition of those who benefited from the old system, and physical attacks were not uncommon. The society's 1904 report noted that "the drawing of weapons and the slashing with knives" had not disappeared. Nor were the new protections yet foolproof. One party of thirty-six immigrants lost seventeen of its number to runners, even with the escort of society guides.[18] These jobs were not for the fainthearted.

By 1904, the society's programs had reduced the average cost of bringing immigrants and their baggage from landing areas to New York destinations from $4.50 per person to thirty-four cents. Society pressure on municipal authorities soon led to the assignment of extra police, some of whom were Italian-speaking, to the Barge area.[19] A municipal ordinance quickly followed, which required the licensing of all runners. By 1906, Speranza and his fellow workers could take justifiable pride in the substantial strides they had taken to provide for the protection of immigrants.

Closely allied to these efforts was a galaxy of other services designed to make further inroads into the hordes of confidence men who preyed upon the newly arrived. The society offered money-transmittal services for Italians anxious to send funds back to the home village. Previously, immigrants lost thousands of dollars annually to dishonest bankers and steamship agents who charged excessive fees for transmittal services. Less fortunate newcomers fell victim to charlatans who claimed all money had been "lost in the mails" while pocketing the sums.[20] The transmission of funds by the society was accomplished at an information bureau run by J. R. Vaccarelli. His staff aided immigrants who had lost baggage, assisted persons who required railroad tickets, directed sick travelers to hospital facilities, and exchanged money. Those in need could also obtain clothing, letter-writing services, information on how to locate relatives, and temporary care of children. Affairs of the heart received society attention as well: picture brides who had never seen their intended mates were often discharged into the hands of the society in order to secure their admittance into the New World. Lastly, the bureau posted lists of approved boarding houses throughout New York and in the major ports of Italy.[21]

The vagaries of the migration process often necessitated temporary stays of two or three days' duration as immigrants attempted to reach inland destinations. At first, the society established a cooperative arrangement with the Italian Benevolent Institution, a church-sponsored charity that supplied housing and food. Some degree of squabbling marred this arrangement and provided opponents of the society with an opportunity for criticism.[22] Consequently, in 1908, the society acquired a building of its own that could be used for office space and lodging. The five-story structure located at 9 Water Street contained dining room, kitchen, washroom, and dormitory facilities for 180 persons. A rate of fifty cents per day included escort service from Ellis Island, three meals, and lodging. Rent for the facility was underwritten by the Italian Government.[23]

By that date, the society was also sponsoring night schools for adults, a kindergarten for children, two loan libraries that circulated in the immigrant districts, and an Italian theater. Occasional efforts were made to bring traveling schools to the sites of large work projects that employed Italians. For the most part, society programs aimed at direct relief of specific problems and avoided the moralistic approaches of other social-service agencies in the city. An exception to this rule consisted of several half-hearted attempts to alter the alleged Italian proclivity for violence. Efforts "against the knife and revolver habit," however, never went beyond the level of exhortations. Periodic efforts to curb the drinking of alcoholic beverages made an appearance as well. One such campaign witnessed the distribution of thousands of pledge cards that read: "I promise for one month, that is from _____ to _____, to abstain absolutely from whiskey and not to use beer except with my meals and that only in the ordinary quantity, one bottle."[24] These crusades, however, were not the core of the society's concern, and were restricted to the fringe of its programs.

Residing fully at the center of the society's mission was a task that the directors regarded as of paramount importance—an attack on the Italian padrone system.[25] For years, labor agents (padroni) had been serving as middlemen between American employers and immigrant workmen. New York was the great national center of these men, and the city itself served as a huge clearinghouse for Italian labor. Each year, padroni recruited, organized, and shipped off to work thousands of men to sites in nearly every corner of North America. The range of abuses laid at the feet of padroni was legion.

Among the thousands of cases that could be cited, one typical incident will suffice. Banca Termini, an immigrant bank located at 3 Mulberry Street in New York City, advertised opportunities for construction work in Pittsburgh. These ads attracted a small party of Italians, who paid a job-finding fee (*bossatura*) and travel expenses to take them to the job site. On April 1, 1906, they left New York for what was to be a short trip to their destination. They arrived in Spruce Plains, North Carolina, two days later, in a bedraggled condition and, for the most part, out of money. Foremen who met the group divided the men into smaller parties and sent them to various work camps. One contingent joined ninety-three other Italians who had arrived by other means, and they journeyed to camp No. 3, where they all suffered severe treatment. Bosses whipped Italians who refused to work, refused them mail from their families, compelled them to spend their entire salaries on food and supplies, subjected them to armed patrols, and threatened to arrest anyone who tried to leave. Ultimately, several men escaped from the camp and made their way back to New York, where they reported the plight of the remaining Italians.[26]

As a remedy, the society proposed to establish its own labor bureau that would find suitable employment for immigrants at a standardized, low fee. What was accomplished in the campaign against runners, the society believed, could be duplicated in this effort against the padrone. Speranza again played a leading role in directing the society's work and in providing important perspectives on the immigrant world. While he decried the abuses of the system, he realized that the padrone served a significant function in the Italian migration process. He was not swayed by nativist critics who saw, in the padrone system, evidence of the backwardness and undesirability of Italian immigrants. Indeed, he was almost alone, among middle-class writers studying Italian immigration, in showing that the migrants themselves seldom urged the abolition of the padrone. Speranza recognized the pivotal role played by the labor agent in providing work opportunities for the temporary sojourners coming to America in search of employment. Hence, he called, not for the eradication of the padrone, but rather for the humanizing of the system. He hoped eventually to introduce reform by supplying a class of honest labor brokers who would replace the unscrupulous individuals so characteristic of the system at that time.[27] In the immediate future, however, he aimed at controlling the worst excesses of padrone operations.

Speranza hoped that the labor bureau would accomplish a second "noble purpose" by acting as an agency of distribution. His writings often focused on an array of social problems that he believed were related to urban congestion. Unsatisfactory conditions of sanitation, health, and living space were intensified, in his view, by the existence of large, tightly packed "Little Italies." Speranza claimed that the padrone system was a prime factor in creating these congested conditions, and if labor agencies could be removed or regulated, settlement patterns would be altered. At his urging, the society's labor bureau required job applicants to accept only out-of-town work.[28] By carefully screening work opportunities and offering only those that held promise of desirable working conditions with fair wages, the society hoped to induce a further movement out of the cities. Once removed from urban colonies, society officials hoped that assimilation would proceed rapidly.

The labor bureau began operations in January 1902, with an office located at 159 Mulberry Street. The society chose Charles B. Phipard, an American agent, as head of the new organization, in a conscious effort to diffuse criticism by American unions. The directors were well aware of organized labor's long record of opposition to any agency that gave the appearance of supporting foreign laborers in America. For his part, Phipard took pains to make clear that his bureau was not attempting to induce immigration or engage in importing contract labor.[29]

In addition to hiring laborers, Phipard attempted to introduce bureau operations into other aspects of the work-camp system. In October 1903, he established a commissary at a large sewer-construction project at Bellmore, Long Island. Hoping to undercut padroni on as many levels as possible, this experiment was to lead the way to the acquisition of other service contracts. However, when the job project terminated earlier than expected, the commissary closed down at a net loss, and no further efforts along those lines were attempted.[30]

Speranza continued to believe that the labor bureau was a key to the society's plans for the betterment of the Italian community. When job-placement totals for the first two years of operations fell far below anticipated levels, he shifted his hopes to schemes designed to settle groups of immigrants in rural colonies. Supporters of the concept urged that immigrants would be attracted to the idea because of the opportunities it offered for mass purchasing power. The impact on relieving urban congestion would be dramatic. Spurred by a visit in 1904 of Adolfo Rossi of the Italian Emigration Department, Speranza himself traveled extensively throughout the South in search of suitable colony and work sites.[31] This trip resulted in a number of solicitations from planters and business-men. One representative offer from a Virginia mining and lumber operation promised twelve thousand acres of land, with small tracts suitable for farming and cottages.[32] Although the energy expended in these efforts was considerable, the overall project was a complete failure. The complexities of arranging travel, construction, and subsistence for such ventures were far beyond the limited capacities of the labor bureau. Moreover, the immigrants themselves resisted the prospect of colonizing in rural America.

Similar failure greeted the more central aspects of the bureau's program. Many of the job offers that came to the central office were from the Deep South (particularly from Alabama and Missis-sippi), and these locations were scorned by immigrants after several peonage scandals captured national headlines.[33] Speranza himself conducted two dramatic investigations of labor conditions in West Virginia, which exposed conditions of appalling brutality and earned national attention. Ultimately, he counseled against sending any Italians to the South, as "the wages are not living wages and even the accommodations offered are inferior."[34] Inadequate oper-ating funds further hindered the ability of the bureau to attract the kinds of contracts that would have ensured its success. A limited advertising campaign organized in 1904 garnered only one contract, and this approach was soon dropped.[35] As the bureau was never able to match the jobs available to the demand, it soon lost support in the immigrant community.

The *prominenti* of the colony, of course, viewed the bureau's work as a direct threat, and they reacted with characteristic vindic-tiveness. "The attacks against the Society and you continue in the Progresso," Speranza wrote to the society president in 1904. "We probably made a mistake in communicating at all with them."[36] Allegations of fraud, deceit, and immorality against the society abounded in the ethnic press, and over time, they effectively sowed seeds of distrust. By 1905, the consul general in New York was sufficiently uncertain of the society's standing that he submitted critical reports to his superiors.[37]

Despite some misgivings about accepting funds from the Italian Government, Speranza had worked hard to maintain strong ties with Italian agencies. In part, this resulted from his deep distrust of indigenous community institutions, which Speranza considered hopelessly controlled by bankers and contractors. Such was his concern to retain Italian connections that he consented to travel to Italy in 1904 on a society mission. The trip was occasioned by the resignation of Senator Luigi Bodio of the Italian Department of Emigration. Bodio had been a strong supporter of the society and its programs and was the moving force behind the government's financial subsidy. So seriously was his departure viewed by the society that Speranza crossed the Atlantic to meet with appropriate government officials and leaders of various philanthropic organizations to secure permanent support. As Sara Wool Moore explained the mission, "We want to send him to the other side where he can answer inquiries, give information, straighten out *misrepresentations* (of which there are many). . . ."[38]

Once in Italy, Speranza discovered that the work of the society was either unknown or regarded with an unfriendly eye. The Foreign Ministry was openly hostile because of negative reports submitted by the consul general in New York. Equally damaging was "a certain popular writer [who] attacked the Society and especially its President in a leading Italian paper." Considerable sentiment existed in the government for a cessation of subsidy payments to the society. Speranza visited all major governmental departments and key members of Parliament in his effort to restore confidence. He visited newspapermen as well, and completed his trip with an audience with the king, who was reportedly "informed of the opposition and criticisms against us." Gino returned on February 16, 1905, and submitted a lengthy report, with recommendations for policy changes.[39] His efforts, however, went unrewarded as the Italian Government withdrew its financial support.

Soon after Speranza returned to the United States, lingering disputes with society president Eliot Norton came to a head. Gino's constant advocacy of the labor bureau's central importance—despite the fact that it was increasingly losing money and draining society finances—was the prime cause of friction. An exchange of letters in April 1905 confirmed the rupture. Norton confessed that the labor bureau was at the heart of the matter—if a success could be made of this project, "all other troubles would settle themselves." Yet he maintained that he was "wholly incapable" of carrying out this campaign any longer. Speranza's resignation from the society's board of directors occurred almost simultaneously with the collapse of the labor bureau.[40]

Cut loose now from the agency that had occupied his energies for the past five years, Speranza put his considerable talents to work in other directions. He again used his connections with Italy. The 1901 Emigration Law of Italy had provided finances to be used for the benefit of immigrants abroad. To utilize these funds, the Emigration Department decided to create an office in New York City, with the express purpose of safeguarding the interests of Italians in that consular jurisdiction. On February 15, 1906, out of these plans emerged the Investigating Bureau for Italian Immigrants. Speranza filled the roles of director and chief investigating attorney for the bureau, which occupied offices at 226 Lafayette Street.[41]

The new director hoped to use his office as a central receiving agency for complaints. Cases of industrial-safety negligence, fraudulent estate settlement, and labor abuses—to name a few—were to be investigated by his small staff of legal assistants and prosecuted through the courts. Individual immigrants rarely possessed the resources, information, or confidence to utilize these avenues of recourse on their own. That the services offered by the Investigating Bureau were effective is testified to by the large volume of cases that are recorded in the Speranza Papers.[42] Problems of budget and staff, however, kept the bureau from expanding its operations.

In an effort to increase the Investigating Bureau's effectiveness, Speranza attempted to connect its operations with those of a new agency in the city. When the Italian Government withdrew its support of the society's labor bureau, it searched for a substitute. The solution was to establish an independent labor office completely under outside control. With an initial grant of $30,000, a Labor Information Office for Italians was opened in April 1906.[43] The office was designed to supply the same types of labor services previously offered by the society, but with its control and operating funds placed above the internal squabbles of the local Italian colony, supporters hoped for better results.

Speranza concurred with the Information Office's mandate requiring employment out of the city and its restriction against offering employment in a strike situation. Indeed, he worked with the agency in the capacity of attorney to the board of directors. Yet his proposals requesting a sharing of expenses in investigating work were rebuffed. The Information Office was willing to intervene only in cases involving workers who had been placed through its services.[44] Because of the very nature of the safeguards established by the agency, this number was very small.

As in the case of its predecessor, the Information Office soon came under attack by padroni and their allies, who created the same web of deceits to scare away workers. Few of the unskilled workers who were in heavy demand registered at the office. Placements never exceeded six thousand in any year of the office's existence; given the annual number of immigrants, this was an inconsequential number. Totals dwindled to such an extent by 1911 that the Italian Government withdrew its support and turned to the now-reorganized (and renamed) Society for Italian Immigrants.[45] Society personnel made efforts to continue placement work, with decreasing rates of success, until 1919, when the labor office closed permanently.[46]

The fact that the padrone system was able to survive repeated attacks during these years is testimony to its amazing resiliency and durability. In the end, the demise of the system depended far more on changes within the ethnic group itself and on alterations in the national economy than on the efforts of reformers. Yet the labors of men such as Speranza were not totally in vain: the sheer volume of investigative reports, speeches, published essays, and documents that he produced served an important role in educating the American public and immigrants to dangers inherent in the system. Much of the data underpinning the successful drafting of a New York law requiring the licensing of all labor agents came from the writings of Speranza.[47] Even while padrone operations continued, the more exploitative aspects of this commerce in labor were ameliorated.

In 1912, Speranza gave up his successful law practice to concentrate more fully on his writing career and to provide additional time for volunteer activities. He quickly became more heavily involved with the affairs of the *Scuola d'Industrie Italiane*, a lace and embroidery crafts school begun by him and his wife in 1905. The founders envisioned the *scuola* as a vehicle for presenting a "more valuable and appealing side of our Italian immigration" to Americans while at the same time preserving ancient craft skills that were fast disappearing. On a more practical level, the school was to rescue immigrant women from the evils of factory and sweatshop work. Modeled after similar schools in Italy with which the Speranzas were familiar, and begun with the technical expertise of Italian teachers, the *scuola* enjoyed prosperity during its early years. The year 1912 witnessed a financial crisis that almost forced the school to close its doors. Gino headed a committee to study the situation, which blamed the difficulties on bad management. Ultimately, reductions in expenses and changes in organization allowed the *scuola* to continue operating until 1927 (quite possibly the longest-lived such experiment in America).[48]

Speranza's literary plans called for the preparation of "a systematic interpretation of Italy to America and of America to Italy."[49] He had already laid an impressive foundation for such a study. During the preceding years, he had investigated many different aspects of the Italian immigration experience. In general, these efforts were designed to make the Italian influx more comprehensible—and hence less threatening—to Americans. A series of articles published from 1904 to 1906, for example, attempted to explain Italian cultural attitudes toward charity work and hospitals. Other essays discussed alterations in the Italian family structure encountered in America, particularly in the relationships of women and work. Speranza had never shied away from the unpleasant in his essays: several short studies dealing with crime, the Black Hand, and the Mafia image still have value today.[50] Perhaps the most perceptive of these early works, however, were those that attempted to explain the nature of immigrant institutions in America. Speranza patiently outlined to American readers the backgrounds and workings of mutual-aid societies, Italian-language newspapers, immigrant banks, and religious festivals.[51]

Except for a few short items published in 1913 and 1914, Speranza's ambitious writing program was curtailed by the advent of World War I. Shortly after the beginning of hostilities, he began to write free-lance articles on the state of public opinion in Italy. When Italy joined the war effort as an active participant in 1915, he journeyed to the peninsula as a feature correspondent for the *New York Evening Post* and *The Outlook*. In that capacity, he authored over sixty articles describing the little-known Italian front for Americans. Many of them were composed while Speranza shared front-line dangers with the soldiers. In April 1917, he volunteered to work with the American ambassador in Rome in the office of the military attaché. Shortly thereafter, he was given an official appointment by the secretary of state, becoming an attaché on political intelligence at the embassy.[52] He came to know the experience of war on every level, from the muddy trenches of the Isonzo front to the carpeted rooms of official Rome.

Speranza's cultural pluralism was transformed during the war. Earlier, in 1905, he wrote with obvious passion to a friend on the subject of assimilation. "While I believe in assimilation and Americanization of the Italian here," he explained, "I believe in an intelligent Americanization. . . . I think that any Italian will be an infinitely better American citizen if, while developing under the best American influences, the ideals of Italian life, which have been the ideals of civilization, are fostered and developed in him at the same time." "Indeed, I feel that I would fail in my duty as an American," Speranza continued, "if I participated in a work which tended to make an Italian ashamed of or indifferent to his Italian antecedents."[53]

Although they appeared on no casuality lists, the pluralist views of his younger days had been destroyed by the war and its aftermath. The catalyst that produced these changes appears to have been President Woodrow Wilson's bruising fight with Italy over the issue of Fiume. Up to that time, Speranza had enjoyed immense popularity in Italy as a gifted correspondent and as a representative of Italy's favorite ally. This friendliness came to an abrupt halt in March 1919, when tensions over President Wilson's stand against Italian claims to Fiume and other territories boiled to a fever pitch. Speranza was attacked viciously in the Italian press, which accused him of being, among other things, "a paid agent of Jugo-Slav imperialism" and a ruthless Americanizer of Italians in New York.[54] By his own testimony, he now began to suspect that the differences between Italians and Americans might be more profound and potentially irreconcilable than he imagined. These doubts occasioned a thorough reassessment of his previous beliefs regarding assimilation and the role of foreigners in American society. Speranza returned home in May 1919, determined to pursue a rigorous examination of his newly found views.

Speranza published the results of his reflections in *Race or Nation: A Conflict of Divided Loyalties*, a book-length study that appeared in 1923. He explained that he had previously believed America's assimilating powers could incorporate many different heritages. But "long study, observation, and thought have wholly changed my views." He now maintained that America was unable to absorb large numbers of foreign immigrants—including, of course, Italians—and the nation was faced with the critical problem of "mass alienage." America could no longer support the inclusion of "huge blocks of foreign stocks...pouring in unabsorbable masses into a nation, already fully formed and grown to manhood." Something of a mutual incompatibility existed in this situation. On the one hand, America had presumably lost its youthful capacity to merge immigrants into an ever-expanding society. At the same time, the foreigners themselves appeared more resistant to integration into America's success story of progress and advancement. If immigration were allowed to continue, the nation's future was in grave peril.[55]

As an alternative to present policies, Speranza offered a four-point program to "rescue America." First, he urged the cessation of all further immigration (with provisions allowing the admittance of close relatives). Second, Speranza advocated that laws be changed to require twenty years of residence before naturalization. Next, a constitutional amendment was necessary to ensure a common language (English) and a universal American public-school system. The schools were to become "a national institution under some form of national authority." This recommendation also included provisions for excluding from public office and the franchise anyone who did not read and write English, requirements mandating the expulsion of foreign languages from public-school curriculums, and stipulations calling for the suppression of the foreign-language press. (This was Americanization with an iron hand!) Finally, Speranza urged that a federal racial census or national ethnological survey be conducted to provide the data necessary for drafting new legislation. New laws written on the basis of this work were to insure "conformity to the American spirit, to American life and history, to American ideals and aspirations."[56]

The intellectual odyssey followed by Speranza was, in many ways, a reflection in microcosm of what was then transforming American society. The emotional postwar atmosphere of the "Red Scare," the economic recession, the restrictionist debates, and the lingering "super-patriotism" of the war years all had their effect on man and nation. It is perhaps not surprising that his views changed considerably. The wider Progressive reform movement suffered much the same fate. Overtaken by the disillusionment engendered by the war, and increasingly feeling the pressure toward conformity and mass culture that was building in the 1920s, many liberal efforts of the earlier age were driven underground, destroyed, or mutated. In this sense, Speranza's conversion to total Americanization can be viewed as symptomatic of a larger national pattern that culminated in the national Origins Act of 1924 and in the revival of the Ku Klux Klan.

Yet, the mystery remains. What caused this sensitive man to undergo such a revolution in thought? We cannot know for certain, since he never fully described the paths leading him to his new beliefs. There is little doubt, however, that the searing experience of World War I, with its previously unimagined brutality and suffering, gave him cause for reflection. For Speranza and many others the inhuman excesses of the war revealed dramatically the extremes that resulted from unbridled nationalism. Events were made more personal for Speranza when essentially nationalistic issues led to the estrangement of the United States and Italy after the war. The thought slowly crystalized in his mind that perhaps national traits and characteristics were not so malleable as he had once believed. If true, was not America, with its heterogeneous population mix, in danger? Ultimately, Speranza was to answer this query with an emphatic affirmative.

On a different level Speranza's experience points out the difficulty individuals encountered during the Progressive era in understanding the workings of the migration process. For the most part, available scholarship and social analysis explained only imperfectly the dynamics of immigration, and not infrequently with racist overtones. Even the sympathetic observer was often unable to comprehend the long view of immigrant development. This explains, at least partially, why most Progressive efforts to shape Italian America failed, except in superficial ways. Perhaps, then, the disillusionment Speranza felt over his inability to perceive more "progress" in the immigrant community reflected his contemporary appreciation of the unfolding process of migration, settlement, and assimilation. Nor was he alone in his gloomy assessment of Italian and other immigrant adaptations to America. No less a scholar than Robert Foerster, who wrote in 1919 what is still the best single volume examination of Italian immigration, came to a very somber conclusion regarding the status and future of Italian newcomers.

That both men wrote in the midst of this great folk movement accounts for much of their pessimism.

Speranza's career also demonstrates the need to view reform efforts aimed at immigrants in the context of the group itself. Analyses of competing solutions to immigrant exploitation have all too often failed to recognize the role played by immigrants themselves. Italians defined much of the adjustment process they underwent in the New World, and by doing so, they made their adaptation distinct from that undergone by other immigrant groups. They resisted, for example, prospects of colonizing in rural America and were reluctant to forego use of the padroni as reformers would have wished them to do. These people were not passive agents awaiting the dictates of the host society or of selected individuals within the immigrant community. Instead they were actors who shaped their futures based upon the new conditions they found in America and the cultural and institutional baggage they brought with them from Italy.

The assimilationist position held by Speranza at the end of his life should not obscure the work he had accomplished on behalf of Italian immigrants. Certainly, during his early career, he was able to avoid the racist and/or religious stereotypes of the age and concentrate on practical reforms that affected immigrants in direct ways. He rejected agendas of social control that so characterized other social welfare agencies at work in America. To accomplish his goals, he was willing, and frequently able, to enlist the aid of the Italian government. This alone was no small accomplishment, given the distrust shown by immigrants toward the Italian government and the previous record of reform efforts supported by the homeland. In this respect, Speranza's work points out the need to look more closely at the international context of immigration reform activity. Speranza not only wrote of reform needs, but he also created and implemented institutional strategies to carry out his conceptions. Such organizations as the Society for the Protection of Italian Immigrants played a role in the developing immigrant community that produced meaningful results. In the end, Speranza's many efforts succeeded in making the condition of Italian immigrants who came to America safer and more humane. Such considerations should not be taken lightly.

Speranza does not fit comfortably into the standard reform typologies. His paradoxical career saw him as a man in between—

someone who shared in both the native and the immigrant worlds. As such, he was often a man at war with himself, as evidenced by his journey along a continuum stretching from cultural pluralism to Americanization. The competing ideologies and loyalties that whipsawed Speranza during his lifetime illustrate the problems inherent in using historical labels—progressive, reformer, nativist, and so on—to describe the complex reality that was this man. To the extent that Speranza may have been representative of other individuals emersed in the world of immigrants, his life offers a different perspective on—and potentially a new typology of— immigrant reform activity.

NOTES

1. Alexander Johnson, *Adventures in Social Welfare: Being Reminiscences of Things, Thoughts and Folks During Forty Years of Social Work* (Fort Wayne, Ind., 1923), and Mary E. Richmond, *Friendly Visiting Among the Poor* (New York, 1899). Excellent discussions of settlement house and social work are contained in Allen F. Davis, *Spearheads for Reform: The Social Settlements and the Progressive Movement, 1890-1914* (New York, 1967), and Roy Lubove, *The Professional Altruist: The Emergence of Social Work as a Career, 1880-1930* (New York, 1969). Also see Walter I. Trattner, *From Poor Law to Welfare State: A History of Social Welfare in America* (New York, 1974).

2. Raymond A. Mohl and Neil Betten, "Paternalism and Pluralism: Immigrants and Social Welfare in Gary, Indiana, 1906-1940," *American Studies* 15 (Spring 1974): 5. Also see Ralph E. Pumphrey, "Compassion and Protection: Dual Motivations in Social Welfare," *Social Service Review* 33 (March 1959): 22.

3. Florence C. Speranza, *The Dairy of Gino Speranza: Italy, 1915-1919*, 2 vols. (New York: Columbia University Press, 1941), 1: x-xi; *New York Times*, July 13, 1927 (obituary); and *Corriere della Sera*, June 19, 1911 (obituary of father).

4. *Corriere della Sera*, June 1, 1912, and Speranza, "The Problem of the Immigrant—An International One," *Charities* 14 (1905): 1063-66.

5. Gino C. Speranza, "The Foreigner Before Our Courts," National Conference of Charities and Corrections, *Proceedings* 36 (1909): 239.

6. "The Interpreter in Our Courts," typewritten copy, 11 pages, p. 4, Gino C. Speranza Collection, New York Public Library, N.Y. For other observations on the court system, see Speranza to Carl L. Schurz, June 27, 1905.

7. Ibid., p. 11.

8. First Preliminary Report of Investigation of Notaries Public," type-written, 6 pages, p. 4, Speranza MSS.

9. *New York Evening Post*, Oct. 13, 1900, and Gino C. Speranza, "The Handicaps of Immigration," *The Survey* 25 (1910):471. For a perceptive examination of the ways in which immigrants used to structure a new social order for themselves, see Robert Harney, "*Ambiente* and Social Class in North American Little Italies," *Canadian Review of Studies in Nationalism* 2 (Spring 1975):208-24.

10. "The Meanest Fraud of All," handwritten notes, and Speranza to Luigi Bodio, May 5, 1904, Speranza MSS.

11. For more information on these early efforts, see George E. Pozzetta, "The Italians of New York City, 1890-1914" (Ph.D. diss., University of North Carolina, 1971), pp. 232-47, and Edwin Fenton, *Immigrants and Unions, A Case Study: Italians and American Labor, 1870-1920* (New York, 1975), pp. 31-95. Also consult Speranza, "America Arraigned," *Survey* 33 (1914-15): 84-86.

12. Constitution of the Society for the Protection of Italian Immigrants (New York, 1901), p. 17, copy in Speranza MSS. Also see "The Society for the Protection of Italian Immigrants," *Charities* 9 (1902):177-78; *New York Tribune*, May 10, 1901.

13. Eliot Norton to Luigi Bodio, June 17, 1901; Gino Speranza to Alice Aspinwall, Apr. 20, 1904; Speranza to Mrs. Lorillard Spencer, Mar. 8, 1904; and Speranza to Miss Dreier, Apr. 26, 1906, Speranza MSS.

14. Joseph T. Keiley to Speranza, Apr. 21, 29, 1901. A group of Catholic ladies apparently made claims that the group was "a proselytising Society trying to work under the cloak of non-sectarianism."

15. Speranza to Rossi, (?) 1903, and Speranza to W. Kirkpatrick Brice, Dec. 14, 1905, Speranza MSS.

16. The Society for the Protection of Italian Immigrants, *Second Report, 1902*, p. 3; W. R. Howland to Norton, June 17, 1902; E. T. Hersoby to Speranza, Apr. 15, 1901; and *New York Tribune*, Dec. 23, 1902.

17. The Speranza MSS contain a good example of the dangers, in *How Salvatore Zamanti, an Italian Immigrant, was Swindled: A Series of Documents Published by the Society for the Protection of Italian Immigrants* (New York, 1904). Also see Norton to Speranza, Oct. 4, 1904, Speranza MSS.

18. The Society for Italian Immigrants, *Fourth Report, 1904-06*, p. 4, and *Societa per gli Emigranti Italiani* (New York, March 1905), p. 5. Antonio Giorgio, society representative, reported that in the first year of operation, the service conducted one thousand and seven immigrants to their destinations safely.

19. *New York Times*, July 21, 1903; *New York Tribune*, Feb. 23, Mar. 3, 1903; Speranza, "Solving the Immigration Problem," *Outlook* 76 (1904):929; and T. Dorr, "Protection of Italian Immigrants," *Leslie's Weekly* 108 (1904):14.

20. Speranza, "Handicaps," p. 470, and *Report of the Commission of Immigration*, State of New York (New York: State Printing Office, 1909), p. 27. Speranza served as a member of the Immigration Commission, joining such other noted reformers as Lillian D. Wald, Frances A. Kellor, and Louis Marshall. Also see Saverio Merlino, "Italian Immigrants and their Enslavement," *Forum* 15 (1893):188, and Speranza to George Von L. Meyer, postmaster general, (?) 1906, Speranza MSS.

21. *New York Tribune*, June 15, 1902, Mar. 3, 1903. Circulars describing the society and its services were distributed throughout Italy.

22. Society for the Protection of Italian Immigrants, *Fourth Report, 1904-06*, p. 7, and Speranza to Norton, Mar. 9, 1904, Speranza MSS.

23. Umberto Coletti, "The Italian Immigrant," National Conference of Charities, *Proceedings* 29 (1912): 250, and The Society for Italian Immigrants, *Seventh Report, 1908-1909*, n.p.

24. *Seventh Report, 1908-09*. During a Mediterranean cholera epidemic, the society sent an interpreter to help Italians who had been placed in quarantine in various countries.

25. Speranza, "The Assimilation of Immigrants," undated speech, Speranza MSS. "Labor Abuses Among Italians," *Charities* 12 (1904): 448-49; Eliot Norton to Giovanni Branchi, Dec. 23, 1901; and *New York Times*, Oct. 11, 1903. For an interpretative assessment of the padrone system, see Robert Harney, "The Padrone and the Immigrant," *Canadian Review oj American Studies* 5 (Fall 1974): 101-18.

26. Typed affidavit dated April 1906, in Speranza MSS.

27. Speranza, "The Italian Foreman as a Social Agent," *Charities* 11 (1903):27, and Speranza, "The Italian in Congested Districts," *Charities and the Commons* 20 (1908):55.

28. Speranza, "The Problem of Immigration Is Only One of Distribution," *New York Sunday News*, Feb. 23, 1902, clipping; Lydio Patrizie to Speranza, June 19, 1902; Speranza, "The Industrial and Civic Relations of the Italian in Congested Districts," typewritten copy in Speranza MSS; and Speranza, "The Italians in the United States," *Chautauquan* 9 (1888-89):347.

29. Charles Phipard to Eliot Norton, Dec. 5, 1904, Speranza MSS.

30. Speranza, "The Italian Emigration Department in 1904," *Charities and the Commons* 11 (October 1905): 114-16, and Speranza, "A Mission of Peace," *Outlook* 78 (September 1904):128-31.

31. Speranza to H. Ellis, Mar. 16, 1904, and Speranza to Thurston J. Allen, Apr. 28, 1904, Speranza MSS.

32. Great Southern Coal and Iron Co. to Speranza, May 10, 1904. Also see C. B. Phipard to Norton, July 28, 1904; Hugh MacRae and Co. to Speranza, June 1, 1905; and L. Ellis to Speranza, May 10, 1904, Speranza MSS.

33. Norval D. Kemp to Speranza, Oct. 6, 1908; C. B. Phipard to J. H. Humpe, May 4, 1904; and W. A. Moyer to Speranza, Apr. 8, 1904, Speranza MSS. A large number of requests were also received from western states for coal miners.

34. Speranza to Elizabeth C. MacMartin, May 9, 1904; Speranza, "Forced Labor in West Virginia," *Outlook* 74 (1903): 407-10; and report to Conte A. R. Massiglia, consul general, May 25, 1906, typewritten, 9 pages, Speranza MSS.

35. C. B. Phipard to Norton, Nov. 29, 1904, Speranza MSS.

36. Speranza to Norton, Mar. 9, 1904. Also see Speranza to Celestino Piva, May 3, 1904, Speranza MSS. Several *prominenti* lodged formal charges with U.S. Immigration Commissioner William Williams against the society. His investigation completely exonerated the society from any wrongdoing.

37. Sara W. Moore to Speranza, Sept. 13, 1904; J. H. Canfield to Speranza, Oct. 27, 1904, Speranza MSS; and *New York Times*, Mar. 22, 1903.

38. S. W. Moore to L. J. Chamberlain, Aug. 11, 1904, and S. W. Moore to Speranza, Sept. 1, 1904. Speranza sailed on November 2, 1904, aboard the *Liguria*.

39. "Report on the Mission to Italy to the Directors of the Society for Italian Immigrants," April 1905, typewritten copy, 14 pages, Speranza MSS. He received the assistance of the U.S. ambassador and certain friendly Italian senators, and was permitted to present reports on the padrone system and the society's labor bureau to several parliamentary committees.

40. Norton to Speranza, Apr. 29, 1905; J. H. Canfield to Speranza, Apr. 18, 20, 29, 1905; and Speranza to Paul U. Kellogg, Oct. 21, 1905, Speranza MSS.

41. Speranza to Frank J. Warne, Aug. 29, 1906, and "Work and Rules of Investigating Bureau for Italian Immigrants," broadbill dated February 1906, Speranza MSS.

42. Memorandum for Italian consulate, "Statement of Facts," dated 1912, Speranza MSS.

43. "The Labor Information Office for Italians," *Charities and the Commons* 16 (1906):402-03, and "Labor Information Office for Italians," broadbill dated Apr. 9, 1906, Speranza MSS.

44. Speranza to G. Rosati, general manager, Labor Information Office, May 11, 1906, Speranza MSS.

45. Fenton, *Immigrants and Unions*, pp. 127-28.

46. Society for Italian Immigrants, *Thirteenth Report, 1917-1919*, p. 5. The *Report* for 1915 indicated that only 807 men had been placed during the year.

47. "The Padrone Must Go," *Immigrants in America Review* 1, (1915):8. Speranza's works almost certainly served to defuse at least some of the criticism directed against Italians due to the padrone system.

48. George E. Pozzetta, "Immigrants and Craft Arts: Scuola d'Industrie Italiane," in Betty Caroli et al., eds., *The Italian Immigrant Woman in North America* (Toronto, Multicultural History Society, 1978), pp. 138-53, contains the full story of the *scuola*.

49. F. C. Speranza, *Diary*, 1:xiii.

50. *New York Evening Post*, July 29, 1904, Apr. 13, 1905, May 5, 1906; "Strife Due to Immigrants," typewritten copy; "Report to American Institute of Criminal Law and Criminology," typewritten copy; Speranza, "The Mafia," *The Green Bag* 12 (June 1900):302-05; and Speranza, "Petrosino and the Black Hand," *The Survey* 22 (1909):11-14.

51. "Italian Characteristics," handwritten speech; "Some Aspects of the Immigration Problem," typewritten copy; "The Bright Side in the Life of our Immigrants," typewritten, 9 pages; Speranza, "Solving the Immigration Problem," *Outlook* 77 (1904):928-33; and *New York Times*, Mar. 8, 1903.

52. F. C. Speranza, *Diary*, 1:xv-xvi. Just before the war, Speranza had visited Florence and discovered the manuscript file of Fillipo Mazzei, which he annotated. He was to use these materials for a projected study of the Italians in colonial Virginia.

53. Speranza to W. Kirkpatrick Brice, Dec. 14, 1905.

54. F. C. Speranza, *Diary*, 2:275; "Fiume and New York," broadbill signed by Speranza, Speranza MSS.

55. Speranza, *Race or Nation: A Conflict of Divided Loyalties* (Indianapolis: Bobbs-Merrill Co., 1923), pp. 31, 71. Some of these ideas can be traced in "Does Americanization Americanize?" *Atlantic Monthly*, 125 (1920):263-69, and "Racial Hygiene in the United States," *The Survey* 30 (1913):656-60.

56. Speranza, *Race or Nation*, pp. 240-65.

4

MUCKRAKING THE MUCKRAKERS: UPTON SINCLAIR AND HIS PEERS[1]

Judson A. Grenier

Upton Sinclair has been called, variously, "king of the muck-rakers," "the original muckraker" (in the sense that President Theodore Roosevelt had Sinclair in mind when he delivered his famous 1906 speech on the topic), and the "last remaining muck-racker."[2] Sinclair himself would have rejected those accolades. His career was closely associated with the muckraking movement of the Progressive era (1899-1916), but it had certain unique characteristics. He was not a working journalist. He was younger than the other reformers and viewed society from the perspective of a different generation.[3] His work was much more personal and probably more ideologically committed than was the work of most of the others.

Sinclair knew that he was on the fringe rather than at the heart of the fraternity of newspaper and magazine reporters and editors who, for nearly twenty years, exposed to the public eye the excesses and foibles of American business and politics. The reformist press tended to treat him with an air of condescension. The men and women who had attained a modicum of fame by rising through the intensely competitive strata of big-city journalism at the turn of the century did not readily embrace newcomers who had not proved themselves in the same arena. Detached from the press, yet associated with it, Sinclair was in a singular position to observe and analyze its behavior and, finally, to muckrake the press itself, as he did in the 1919 volume, *The Brass Check*.

Sinclair's relationship to the profession of journalism was close, and highly ambivalent throughout his lifetime. His novels were journalistic in tone and content, the characters often thinly disguised portraits of living political and economic leaders. Newspapers and magazines provided most of the grist for his creative mill; his files bulged with clippings from a vast variety of journals. His quest for "social justice" was generated largely by press revelations of corruption and persecution. In the impressionistic years of his early teens in New York City, Sinclair regularly followed the reformist campaigns of E. L. Godkin's *Evening Post* and Charles A. Dana's *Sun* against a rotten urban political system that linked criminals, government, liquor dealers, police, and prostitutes. For two weeks in 1894, at age sixteen, Sinclair was a member of the *Post* staff, but he resigned after being assigned a steady diet of obituaries.[4] His career as a reporter was at an end.

Sinclair turned his talents to fiction: short stories, escapist children's tales, poetry, and serials. His early novels, published between 1901 and 1904, emphasized imagination rather than reality and tended toward the sentimental.[5] But his conversion to socialism in 1904 led him back to a more journalistic approach in order to address more effectively a working-class audience. Articles by Sinclair on the socialist movement appeared in *Appeal to Reason*, a large-circulation journal published in Kansas, and in *Collier's Magazine*, in late summer of 1904. On assignment for *Appeal*, Sinclair visited the Chicago meatpacking industry in November and December of 1904, and from intensive interviews with workers, lawyers, bar owners, doctors, and their families, he created the novel that was serialized in *Appeal* in 1905 as *The Jungle*.[6] It gave him notoriety at age twenty-seven and was popular, in part, because its publication coincided with a campaign against food adulterants and poisons being mounted by Dr. Harvey Wiley of the Department of Agriculture, by Progressive politicians, and by the press.[7]

The Jungle appeared while the muckraking movement in journalism was in full flower. Sinclair's new fame won him access to newspaper and magazine offices. He maintained an almost confidential relationship with scores of reporters and editors; they told him anecdotes that the press would not use, and Sinclair adapted them to fiction. According to Sinclair, "There's always some man who has enough conscience left to know that it's crooked and... wishes he could do business without doing this or that."[8] Such a man would talk off the record, and if the material could not be adapted to the pages of the *New York Journal* or *McClure's Magazine*, it would become a short story or a socialist tract. Many working reporters sympathized with Sinclair's activist behavior and aided him covertly. He and the working press used each other effectively; he was kept informed of opportunities or dangers, and, in turn, he made colorful copy in crisis situations.[9] Some of Sinclair's novels are little more than collections of interviews and anecdotes told him by newsmen, strung together with a semblance of a plot.[10]

Recalling the turn-of-the-century newspaperman's life, Sinclair wrote:

> The men of that world had very few of them what we call "education"; they had learned reading, writing, arithmetic ...and then gone to work. They knew nothing about the past, and had no vision of the future, no understanding of the causes of anything. What they knew was the world about them, its external aspects which they "wrote up" day by day; when they had "inside" knowledge of anything it meant the intrigues and rascalities of men of power, "bastards" like themselves, except that they had wealth, or the greed and energy to prey upon the wealthy.... When you climbed higher, into the magazine world ... you found a world externally different, but spiritually the same; you had a clean office, with rugs on the floor ... but the members of the staff were the same "bastards," risen by virtue of their ability to judge with greater accuracy what the nameless millions outside would spend their money for.[11]

Of all the newspapers or newspaper chains in which Upton Sinclair might have pursued a successful career, the Hearst press seems most likely. Prior to moving to California, Sinclair had published in *Hearst's Magazine*, and in later life, he wrote syndicated articles and book reviews for Hearst. As a teenager, Sinclair learned from his father to read and admire the editorials of Arthur Brisbane, "the most widely read newspaper editor in America."[12] After the publication of *The Jungle*, Brisbane "took up" the young author. "He invited me to his home and wrote one of his famous two-column editorials about [me]."[13] "Brisbane was an intellectual man. He was a man who knew much more than he put on paper.

He was much more radical than he put on paper. He could descend to my level of radicalism."[14] "...He told me that he drank in Socialism with his mother's milk."[15]

Sinclair also knew the muckraking Hearst reporter Alfred Henry Lewis. He recalled Lewis offering to show him "the real New York!" "...He told me the 'inside story' of New York politics, graft and coruption. Then we began to move from popular spot to popular spot, and he introduced me as we went to one Broadway character after another."[16]

> He was a drinking man himself. He took me into the place where the *Times* building now is. There was a very famous cafe on the ground floor. He introduced me to Tenderloin life —I was with some famous cowboy, listened to him and Lewis talk about all the gangsters and touts. Lewis was a fountain of gossip and chatter. He was a man-about-town, and he took me in tow.[17]

Of all Hearst editors, Sinclair was most intimately acquainted with Charles Edward Russell, who later became both a well-known magazine muckraker and a Socialist. In 1963, Sinclair spoke of Russell with great enthusiasm and respect.

> I used to say that one of the reasons for going to New York was the delight of hearing Charlie Russell cuss the capitalist system. He was an extreme radical—as much so as I was—he hated the big business system like poison and he poured it out whenever we talked together. And so to me he was a very delightful fellow. But after he retired to the country to write, I saw little of him.[18]

Sinclair also was an admirer of Ambrose Bierce, in spite of the fact that Bierce had been critical of him in a number of articles written for Hearst. Sinclair said that Bierce gave the world "love of truth, and loathing of corruption and hypocrisy."[19] On the other hand, he thought little of sobsister "Annie Laurie" (Winifred Sweet), who interviewed him in San Francisco in January 1909 and prodded him into expressing his views on "trial marriages" of five to ten years. Sinclair discussed modern marriage in general and the subservient condition of women; then, he bought Miss Laurie lunch. She was "a pleasant lady who introduced herself as a friend of an old friend of mine." The next day, the *Examiner* ran the interview under the headline "Upton Sinclair Sorry He Wed, Says Ceremony Is Farce." In a local theater that night, Sinclair complained about the interview, and the following day, Annie Laurie "took up the cudgels . . . upbraiding me for 'playing the cry-baby' and refusing to stand by the words that I had spoken . . . She was so vulgar that she saw no difference between the phrases I had used and the twist she had given to them."[20] In *The Brass Check*, Sinclair wrote, "[This] star writer . . . was working on a fancy salary, earned by her ability to cook up sensations, to keep her name and her picture on the front page." She distorted what he said, and the city editor played along, "thus attracting to himself the attention of the heads of the Hearst machine."[21]

With Hearst himself, Sinclair became disillusioned. In 1907, Sinclair wrote a book titled *The Industrial Republic*, a prophecy of socialism in America. "I have never reprinted this book because of the embarrassing fact that I prophesied Hearst as a radical president of the United States. He really looked like a radical then, and I was too naive to imagine the depths of his cynicism and depravity."[22] Sinclair told me that for about twenty-five years, the Hearst newspapers had the appearance of being radical, or at least reformist, because they supported some form of public ownership.[23]

In the early 1900s, Sinclair resented attacks upon Hearst's political ambitions. "Unquestionably a good deal of this denunciation came from vested interests which he had frightened by his radicalism, but, on the other hand, it betrayed a note of personal loathing that was unmistakable. I marvelled at it at the time; but now I think I understand it."[24] After a series of unpleasant personal experiences with the Hearst press, Sinclair grew bitter. Reporters and editors in the *New York Journal* and *American* and *San Francisco Examiner* not only misquoted him but, at various times, broke into his home, stole stories from him, printed scandals about him and his acquaintances, and sent fictitious telegrams over his signature.

By 1919, he had concluded that what Hearst editors call "a nose for news" "means a nose for the millions of pennies which come pouring into the Hearst coffers every day . . . They have been willing again and again to drive perfectly innocent men and women to ruin and suicide.... They have been willing by deliberate and shameful lies, made out of whole cloth, to stir nations to enmity and drive them to murderous war." For fifteen years, the Hearst newspapers were "used as a means of forcing war with Mexico" in order to annex to the United States the vast Hearst land holdings in that country. Furthermore, Hearst posed "as a friend to labor, but he keeps his newspapers on a non-union basis, and when his employees go on strike, he treats them as other corporations treat their strikers."

Yet Sinclair still subscribed to a Hearst newspaper, the *Los Angeles Examiner*, though he knew he was being brainwashed, because "I am an American, and can no more resist sensational headlines printed in a newspaper than a donkey can resist a field of fat clover."[25] When I interviewed him in 1963, he still subscribed.

> I never met Hearst. He wasn't my kind of person.... I don't think Hearst had any sincerity whatever. Hearst set out to make a great stir in the world and build a big newspaper by playing on the discontent of the laboring masses—the discontent of the discontented, so to speak, and I think he was perfectly cynical about it. I never had any interest in meeting him.[26]

Other than the Hearst press, Sinclair maintained contact with a variety of newsmen. He met the "Gibson man" of the New York reporting corps, Richard Harding Davis, only once in his lifetime. Davis appeared at the opening night of the motion-picture version of *The Jungle*. "He had come back from some expedition and was still wearing khaki. I...had an impression of him as a prince among snobs; but when he heard my name, he held my hand and said, 'Ah, now, *you* are a real writer. I only write for money.'"[27] Of the reforming journalists on the West Coast, Sinclair knew well only Fremont Older, editor of the *San Francisco Bulletin*, whom he called "one of the few independent newspaper editors in America."

> Older began as a plain-every-day hireling of privilege, but little by little his mind and his conscience awakened, he took his stand for righteousness in his city, and fought the enemies of righteousness, not merely at the peril of his job, but at the peril of his life. The first time I met Older ... he had just been

> kidnapped by thugs and carried away in an automobile and
> locked under armed guard in a compartment of a sleeping-car
> . . . to this day I remember my consternation.[28]

In later years, Sinclair worked with Older in the campaign to free
Tom Mooney from prison, and frequently wrote to him for advice.

He also used and was used by the *New York Times*. After the
appearance of *The Jungle*, President Theodore Roosevelt appointed a special commission to investigate the Chicago stock-
yards. Commission members wrote a "confidential" report on
what they had seen. Sinclair obtained a copy and took it to the
Times. Here is his description of the affair:

> I was received by C. W. Van Anda, managing editor of the
> "Times"—and never before or since have I met such a
> welcome in a newspaper office. I told them I had the entire
> substance of the confidential report of Roosevelt's investigat-
> ing committee, and they gave me a private room and two
> expert stenographers, and I talked for a few minutes to one
> stenographer, and then for a few minutes to the other stenog-
> rapher, and so the story was dashed off in about an hour. . . .
> They were caught in a whirlwind of excitement, and at one
> o'clock in the morning my story was on the press, occupying a
> part of the front page and practically all of the second page.[29]

(In print, the story was attributed to one of the *Times's*
Washington correspondents.) For several days thereafter, the
Times published Sinclair's material; ". . . having put its hand to the
plough, [it] went a long way down the furrow." Sinclair gave the
Times leads that reporters checked out; the stories were then sold to
other newspapers around the country. Sinclair did not make a cent
out of the experience, but he was troubled to read in the pages of
the *Times* that he was "in the business of muckraking for money."[30]

To Sinclair, the saddest chapter in the history of the reformist
newspaper press was the last—its eventual fate. Many papers, he
told me, began as lively, crusading journals and then were
pressured by advertisers, compromised by business managers, or
purchased outright by enemies of reform.[31] Sinclair's books *The
Brass Check*, *Money Writes*, and *Mammonart* related many examples of reform journalists who were silenced by Big Business inter-

ests. Furthermore, the original owners and editors lost their enthusiasm and were succeeded by more conservative men. A prime example of this development was that of the Scripps papers. Sinclair wrote in 1919:

> There exists a chain of one-cent evening newspapers scattered over the country, the Scripps papers, catering to working-class audiences. They were founded by a real radical and friend of the people, E. W. Scripps, and for a decade or two were the main resource of the workers in many localities. Now E. W. Scripps is a sick man, out of the game, and his eldest son, who runs the papers, is a young business man, interested in the business management of a great property; so in one city after another you see the Scripps papers "toned-down."[32]

The second son of Scripps, Robert, visited Sinclair in Pasadena. He "was another of the very rich, restlessly seeking for a purpose in life." The young Scripps wanted to be a poet and brought his work to the Sinclairs for encouragement. He received some, but apparently not enough, for he abandoned poetry and followed his father into a publishing career and, like his father, died on board his yacht.[33] Sinclair also believed that the Scrippses drank excessively, a habit he attributed to most of the journalists of the period, reformer and cynic alike.[34]

Upton Sinclair was probably better acquainted with magazine writers of the Progressive era than he was with newspapermen chiefly because he was in contact with various periodicals to market his own articles, anecdotes, and fiction. In the autumn of 1902, he was introduced to two men who would become his close friends, Gaylord Wilshire and Lincoln Steffens. His visit with Wilshire grew out of a call at the office of the *Literary Digest*, where he met "a tall, soft-voiced and gentle-souled youth by the name of Leonard D. Abbott; he was a socialist, so he told me, and he thought I might be interested to know something about the movement. He gave me a couple of pamphlets and a copy of *Wilshire's Magazine*."[35]

Reading that material converted Sinclair to socialism. As a new enthusiast, he was invited to dinner by clergyman-reformer George D. Herron, and there met Wilshire, ". . . a small man with a black beard and mustache trimmed to sharp points, and twinkling mischievous eyes—for all the world the incarnation of Mephistopheles, but without the tail. . . .''

> Wilshire had made a fortune in billboard advertising in Los Angeles. . . . He started a weekly; he then brought it to New York and turned it into a monthly. He was spending his money fast, offering prizes such as grand pianos and trips around the world for the greatest number of new subscribers. He had a standing offer of ten thousand dollars to William Jennings Bryan to debate socialism with him . . . the quick-witted editor would have made a monkey of him. Wilshire always insisted that his conversion was purely a matter of intellect; he had become convinced that capitalism was self-eliminating, and that its breakdown was near. But as a matter of fact, a sense of justice and a kind heart had much to do with his crusade. To hear him talk, you would think him a cynical man of the world . . . but his greatest faults were generosity, which made it impossible for him to keep money, and a sort of "Colonel Sellers" optimism, which made him sure he was going to get a lot more at once.[36]

Wilshire and his wife frequently exchanged visits with the Sinclairs. "Mary Wilshire was sort of older sister to me. . . . I wrote for his columns—I remember 'The Toy and the Man,' wherein I poked fun at the desire of grown-up Americans to accumulate quantities of unnecessary material things.'' But eventually, the publisher became involved in an unprofitable gold mine, which drained his financial resources and sapped his energy.

> *Wilshire's Magazine* was a gift from a billboard advertising man with a sense of humor. So long as his money lasted, we all took his gift with thanks; if his gold-mining gamble had succeeded, we would all have made money, and had a still bigger magazine, and everything would have been lovely. But my old friend Gay died in a hospital in New York, all crippled up with arthritis. I missed his fertile mind and his sly, quiet smile.[37]

Sinclair met Lincoln Steffens at the time Steffens's essays "Shame of the Cities" were appearing in *McClure's Magazine*.

Sinclair had written a criticism of the series, "pointing out that the corruption he [Steffens] reported came about because big business bought the politicians or elected them; and that there could never be an end to it until the government owned businesses, especially the public utilities. I sent the article to Steffens. He wrote me that it was the best criticism of his work that he had seen; he wanted *McClure's* to publish it, but they didn't dare to."[38] "But he remained always one of my closest and dearest friends, and we met whenever we were in the same neighborhood."[39]

> He [Steffens] was a short, compactly built man with a rather square face with glasses, and small blue-gray eyes with many wrinkles around them, giving him a quizzical appearance. ... [He] was plainly but neatly dressed, and you would have taken him for a small businessman, or perhaps a college professor.... He had an unusually pleasing voice.... Stef would become eager and excited, and then would check himself. "If I go too fast," he would say, "people won't listen to me. And besides, I may be wrong." He would proceed to put some "ifs" and "buts" into his discourse.... Steffens was, like Herron, a pacifist and moralist first of all. He wanted a revolution, but one of the mind and spirit; he was pained by the thought that it might have to be bloody and violent."[40]

Sinclair told me:

> Steffens couldn't publish my stuff but he gave me priceless information. When I wanted to write a sequel [to *The Jungle*] dealing with Wall Street and its affairs, Stef introduced me to two men who were priceless in my life. One was Samuel Untermyer, who was the highest paid corporation lawyer at that time. Stef had been an old newspaperman for many years. There were men who were fighting a syndicate, fighting each other, and they wanted to give out publicity against the other fellow. When they found a reporter who was honest, who could be depended upon, and if he were told that something was confidential he wouldn't mention it, they used him. A great deal of Stef's muckraking had come through men like that. They gave him information he wanted. The other man was James B. Dill, also a high paid Wall Street lawyer. Dill

had just been made Chief Justice of the Supreme Court of New Jersey; that meant he had retired from the dirty work.[41]

Steffens would acquaint Sinclair with "anyone I wanted to know. He gave me not only the facts, but the atmosphere. He gave me the reassurance; he knew, he had spent his working life as a Wall Street reporter. He would introduce me to the radicals among them and they would speak to me in confidence." To Sinclair, Steffens was "as close a friend as I had in the muckraking world. He came to stay with us."[42]

I asked Sinclair, "Did you consider Steffens a Socialist?

> I think that Steffens was probably 90 percent of a socialist, but for tactical reasons he never gave himself the name. I could afford to give myself the name and did, but I discussed with Steffens all the problems, everything that was in my heart, and I can't recall that he ever disagreed with anything I said about proposals, about remedies, about ultimate decisions or the destiny of the capitalist system. . . . His job was a different one, you see—I was writing books and could take the responsibility, but Steffens was writing for magazines and papers, and he was tactful. He didn't say all that he knew; he let other people talk and asked them questions.[43]

According to Sinclair, Steffens died discouraged. "What broke Stef's heart was the surrender that Woodrow Wilson made to Clemenceau. When Wilson let Clemenceau browbeat him and betrayed the peace, he made the second world war inevitable; both Herron and Steffens knew that and pointed it out to Wilson. I know they both died sad men."[44]

As for the rest of the *McClure's Magazine* "crowd," as Sinclair called them, "they weren't so radical as Stef was."

> There was Ida Tarbell and there was a humorist who wrote Mr. Dooley—Finley Peter Dunne—one of the jolliest and most delightful fellows I ever met; he just bubbled over with fun. His talk was as interesting as his articles. Not every amusing writer is an amusing talker because they don't want to work outside of hours, they keep their jokes for their business hours—but Dunne couldn't talk without laughing or

laugh without saying something funny. I met him at the office and had dinner with him. He poured out his jokes the way Mr. Dooley did. Ida Tarbell I knew quite well. She was a very gracious and sweet woman. She was not anything of a social-ist, I think; she probably was very careful not to commit her-self to me, but she was always very friendly and warm-hearted. She wanted the magazine to publish my article.... Ida Tarbell was a very cautious lady. She exposed all the career of the Rockefellers, but nobody could ever get her to hint that the United States ought to take over the oil industry. I could never get anywhere with her [politically]. I didn't make a per-sonal issue of it—if he or she didn't agree with me, he or she didn't agree; that was all there was to that.[45]

Similar to Miss Tarbell in political attitude was Ray Stannard Baker.

Ray Baker was a very, very conscientious and cautious pro-gressive with touches of conservatism. He didn't want to commit himself beyond a certain point. I had a little farm near Princeton when I was writing *The Jungle* and he came and spent a weekend with us, and I remember sitting around and talking with him. My conversation with people like that in those days consisted of my trying to make socialists out of them. Ray Baker was skeptical.[46]

With William Allen White, Sinclair maintained a long and friendly correspondence. He remembered the Irwin brothers, Will and Wallace, chiefly from spending an evening at their home in a rather condescending atmosphere, a kind of early-day "radical chic." "I was amusing to them as an out-and-out radical and socialist."[47]

Rebuffed by *McClure's*, Sinclair took his articles to *Collier's Magazine*, where he came to know both Robert Collier, the pub-lisher's son, and editor Norman Hapgood.

Robbie Collier was a fashionable young millionaire with a taste for literature and politics in between his drinking bouts. Young writers and illustrators would appear on the scene, and the generous Robbie would invite them to dinner and give them a contract with his magazine and a card to his country club; they would spend their afternoons sipping cocktails in the Hoffman House bar, and in a year or two would know nothing to write about but sports, motor-cars, women's dress and fashionable fornications. I could name a dozen men to whom this happened.[48]

Such a fate might have befallen Sinclair had he been a man of weaker character. As it was, *Collier's* published two of his articles before old Peter Collier vetoed further contributions. Sinclair met him at one of Robbie's dinners. Staff members were discussing articles that Sinclair might undertake when Peter Collier appeared. Collier was "an ex-pack-paddler," who started *Collier's Weekly* "as an advertisement sheet," and became "rich and important; vulgar, ignorant as a child, but kind-hearted, jovial—one of those nice, fatherly old fellows who put their arms about you, no matter who you are."[49] When Collier learned Sinclair's identity and ideas, he sputtered, "Oh, no, no, no, you can't publish anything like that in the magazine—it would ruin it. Where would we get the advertising?... Please don't try putting your ideas in my magazine and scaring away my half million subscribers."[50]

Although *Collier's* was run on a personal basis, editor Norman Hapgood played a major role in leading the magazine into reform journalism. Said Sinclair, "Hapgood wasn't interested in the idea of any economic change—he thought our society was all right except that we had to run it honestly and he thought that was a possibility."[51] In criticism, Sinclair once wrote that Hapgood "spent his editorial time balancing like a tight-rope walker on the narrow thread of truth, occupying himself like a medieval schoolman with finding the precise mathematical or metaphysical dead centre between the contending forces of conservatism and radicalism." But in praise of the ascetic editor, Sinclair mentioned his resignation from *Collier's* rather than submit to pressure from the business side of the magazine.[52]

Everybody's was probably Upton Sinclair's favorite muckraking magazine. It published his article on the "condemned meat industry," Tom Lawson's series on "Frenzied Finance," and numerous exposés by Russell. "To use the ad men's own slang, it was 'a knockout'; the American people showed that more than any other thing in the entire world they wanted to read about how they were

being robbed wholesale."[53] Sinclair occasionally sent along tips or
ideas to *Everybody's* that resulted in new exposés. For example, he
encountered Ben Lindsey, judge of the children's court in Denver,
read the judge's manuscript of his war with organized corruption,
and telegraphed *Everybody's* about it. That magazine sent Harvey
O'Higgins to Denver and had another muckraking serial, "The
Beast and the Jungle."[54] But even *Everybody's* failed to live up to
the expectations of an Upton Sinclair. In 1926, he wrote:

> ... many years ago "Everybody's Magazine" printed a boast-
> ful editorial, listing all the crusades they had carried on for
> the benefit of the people; and I wrote, challenging them to
> point one single practical result which had come of all their
> efforts, to show where they had been able to divert a single
> dollar from the pockets of the rich into the pockets of the
> poor; and "Everybody's" did not take up that challenge nor
> even print it.[55]

And thus, the muckraking movement, for all its fire and fury,
according to Sinclair, did not lead to major, significant reform.

Again, illustrating Sinclair's ambivalence toward the press, he
considered *Munsey's Magazine* crass and commercial, with an
editorial staff that "... lack the wit to understand it, or the conscience to care about it. That is the criterion according to which
Munsey office-boys are selected."[56] Yet he could be fulsome in
praise of Munsey's Bob Davis ("How I blessed him for it") for
introducing him to an Armour foreman who provided the certified
proof that served as the basis for his article on the meatpacking
industry.[57]

Sometimes, a man's most bitter criticisms are reserved for an
individual who meant a great deal to him at an earlier stage in his
life. So it was with Sinclair. As a student at City College of New
York, he helped found a Christian student group, which met after
hours to listen to speakers with reformist ideas. "I was a Christian
boy in those days—Episcopalian, that was the respectable religion.
I got Lyman Abbott, editor of *The Outlook*, to speak to us. He had
liberal ideas and gave us a very intelligent and fine talk. I respected
him tremendously."[58] By 1918, that respect was gone. Abbott had
become a "theological knave" and "clerical crook"; *The Outlook*, though "our most influential religious weekly," was a tool of
Big Business. Sinclair devoted eleven pages of his searing *The*

Profits of Religion to an attack upon Abbott and *The Outlook*, attempting to demonstrate that its pious reformist moralizing was carried on at the same time that the magazine was accepting money from large industrial interests.[59] (That book touched many sensitive nerves: it came back to haunt Sinclair in his campaign for governor, when the press widely quoted excerpts from it.) By 1963, he had mellowed in his remembrance of Abbott. He recalled that the magazine had employed Theodore Roosevelt as a writer when he retired from the presidency, and later it had backed the Progressive party. "I considered the 'Industrial Democracy' it preached to be quite silly," he avowed.[60]

His memories were fonder of a different sort of reform journalist, Bernard Macfadden. Sinclair had stayed at the Macfadden health resort in Battle Creek, Michigan, and had written many articles for Macfadden publications on various diets and regimens. At one time, these articles were his only income. His evaluation of Macfadden:

> Athlete, showman, lecturer, editor, publisher, and health experimenter. . . . To the high-brows he was a symbol of the vulgarity and cheapness of America. And it won't help for me to defend him, because I may also be on that list. I merely state what Macfadden did for me—which was to teach me free, gratis, and for nothing, more about the true principles of keeping well and fit for my work than all the orthodox and ordained physicians who charged me many thousands of dollars for not doing it. . . . My visit to Macfadden took place in 1909—back in the dark ages, before the words "preventive medicine" had even been joined together . . . I met him again when he was sixty; still of the same experimental disposition, he wanted to know what I had learned in twenty years. He then owned a string of magazines and newspapers. . . . He still had his muscles of steel, and would take two packs of cards and tear them in half before your eyes. . . . [He] caused great numbers of men and women to take an interest in their health, and it set up resistance to those forces of modern civilization that were destroying the body.[61]

Another unusual reform journalist was Frank Harris, whom Sinclair met in England prior to World War I. Sinclair was taken to lunch by H. G. Wells at the New Reform Club, where he encountered Harris. He corresponded frequently with him thereafter, particularly after Harris became editor of the muckraking *Pearson's Magazine* in New York. Sinclair called him "possesser of a golden tongue." "Harris would talk about Jesus and Shakespeare in words so beautiful that only those masters could have matched it; but in the midst of his eloquence something would turn his thoughts to a person he disliked, and there would pour from the same throat such a stream of abuse as might have shocked a fallen archangel."[62] The Sinclair-Harris correspondence is rather amusing to read: one preached socialism; the other, sexual liberation. Harris attempted to persuade Sinclair to relate his sexual experiences; instead, he received lectures on the iniquities of man.[63]

The man whom Sinclair believed inspired Roosevelt's muckraking speech was, like himself, a novelist: David Graham Phillips. Phillips had worked for both Pulitzer and Hearst during his career. Sinclair considered him "a sturdy and vigorous personality, who looked at the world about him with his own eyes and really had something to say." In 1924, Sinclair wrote:

> Phillips was eleven years older than myself, but we arrived upon the literary scene together, and I used to meet him now and then in New York. . . . He was the genuine old-fashioned American, the wearer of square-toed shoes and a string tie. I do not mean that I ever saw him in that costume, but that his view of human society was derived from that period. He came from the Middle West, and believed in the simple, small-town democracy he had known there. A man of common sense, he hated all forms of social pretense and finickyness. Like a good American, he respected money and the power of money, but he wanted the people who had this power to behave like sensible human beings, and he was infuriated because they took to putting on "side," getting English butlers and five footmen in livery.[64]

Sinclair reflected later:

> Phillips I knew very well. He had a little apartment in Gramercy Park. A club across the street from the park was the Players, where authors, dramatists and stage people belonged. I joined it for awhile and used to meet Phillips there. He was

very friendly, warm-hearted. He was a little provoked with me because I talked more radicalism than he approved of. I was a socialist. And he probably thought I didn't think as much of his novels as I ought to. As a matter of fact I found them very interesting, but you know how writers are—they are apt to be a little touchy of one another; they'd rather talk to somebody who isn't in the same business because then the element of competition doesn't matter. I tried to make a socialist out of him and maybe that irritated him a little. I don't think he wanted to see the cat quite so clearly as I did. There was a popular drawing and you had to hunt for the cat —once you saw it you couldn't see anything else. And so I had seen the cat and maybe David didn't want to. Anyhow there was a certain amount of rivalry between us. His early death was a shocking thing for me because I really liked him very much.[65]

Sinclair clearly thought Phillips's articles for *Cosmopolitan* entitled "The Treason of the Senate" (not Colonel Mann's *Town Topics*) provoked Roosevelt's "Man with the Muckrake" speech.[66] "The articles were basically sound, though I had the impression that Phillips . . . was longer on adjectives than on facts."[67]

Phillips didn't get his material documented the way I got mine documented, and that was what Roosevelt had in mind. Roosevelt never named me as a muckraker. I had presented him all the evidence he asked for before he pushed meat inspection laws through Congress. So he certainly didn't call me, never meant me, couldn't have meant me, when he said, "the man with the muckrake."[68]

Reminiscing about Theodore Roosevelt delighted Sinclair. He liked to tell college students of his luncheon visit with the president. "The worst muckraker was Roosevelt himself," he insisted.[69] "Phillips in his wildest moment never said anything against the Old Guard senators more extreme than that I had heard Roosevelt say with his own lips at his own luncheon table. . . . The president called the roll of these traitors, and told me what he knew about each one. I sat appalled—what, after all, did Theodore Roosevelt know about me?" But Sinclair soon learned from other newspapermen in Washington that the president's words "were not to be quoted"; if reporters did so, they would be called liars.[70]

In a sense, the president's speech marked the apex of periodical reform journalism; never again did it weave quite the spell that it created prior to 1906. But Sinclair denied that the public simply lost interest in muckraking.

> Suffice it to say that every magazine in the United States that was publishing any statements injurious to big business was either bought up, or driven into bankruptcy, and "the muck-raking era" passed into unwritten history. The public was told that it, the public, had become disgusted with the excesses of the muckrakers; and the public believed that, just as it had formerly believed the muckrakers. The public believes what-ever it is told in print—what else can it believe? It was obvious enough that the "excesses" had been committed by those who made the muck, not by those who raked it.[71]

In 1927, Sinclair bewailed the fact that "there are no indepen-dent magazines of big circulations left in America—they are all 'chains' now . . . all of them run exactly like the department stores and shoe-factory chains, upon the same principles of standardiza-tion and mass production."[72] *Collier's, Everybody's, McClure's, The Cosmopolitan, The American, Wilshire's, Hampton's, Pearson's*—all were gone or offering only trivia or reaction. "When the big magazines were bought up by the 'interests,' we were solemnly assured that the purpose was to put an end to 'scandal-mongering.' But now it appears that the purpose was not to lay the 'muckrake' on the shelf, but merely to turn it against the friends of human progress."[73] All the reform journalists had either retired, sold out to the system, or turned to biography and romance. In 1963, he was a bit more optimistic. "I have hopes for this gener-ation of newsmen," he told me, "I think they've seen the cat."[74] The revival of muckraking as a respectable vocation would appear to bear him out.

NOTES

1. An early version of this paper was read to a meeting of the Pacific Coast branch of the American Historical Association at the University of

Southern California. It is based, in part, on two oral interviews with Upton Sinclair on February 8-9, 1963. Some of what he said had already appeared in print; some of it was new. The material was tape-recorded and, hereafter, will be referred to as "Interview." (Sinclair also commented on reform journalism in letters to me of October 26, 1959; January 23 and 25, February 26, March 27, 1963; and February 1, 1965.)

All of his works are, to some extent, autobiographical, but this is particularly true of *American Outpost* (New York: Farrar and Reinhardt, 1932); *The Autobiography of Upton Sinclair* (New York: Harcourt, Brace and World, 1962); *The Cup of Fury* (Great Neck, N.Y.: Channel Press, 1956); *Love's Pilgrimage* (New York: Vanguard Press, 1929); and Mary Craig Sinclair's *Southern Belle* (New York: Crown Publishers, 1957).

My personal impressions of the man were told in "Upton Sinclair: A Remembrance," *California Historical Society Quarterly* 48, no. 2 (June 1969):165-69, which appeared shortly after his death. All of the above are utilized in this paper, which combines printed sources and oral interviews stretching across a half century. Sinclair was remarkably consistent through the years in his comments about particular individuals.

2. All of these "titles" have been applied frequently to Sinclair. Edward R. Murrow introduced him as "king of the muckrakers" on his "This I Believe" radio program. See *Cup of Fury*, p. 55.

3. The median date of birth for the twenty best-known muckrakers of the Progressive era is January 1, 1868. Sinclair was born on September 20, 1878, a decade later. Editors S. S. McClure and Ida Tarbell were twenty-one years older than he.

4. Interview. See also *Autobiography*, p. 45, and *The Brass Check* (published by the author: Pasadena, 1919; republished by Albert and Charles Boni, 1936; reprinted by the Arno Press), pp. 14-16.

5. William A. Bloodworth, *Upton Sinclair* (Boston: Twayne Publishers, 1977), pp. 44-45.

6. *The Jungle* was published in book form by Doubleday in 1906.

7. Sinclair's notoriety won him an audience with President Theodore Roosevelt. After the two commiserated with one another over being misquoted by the press, the president warned Sinclair, "If you pay any attention to what the newspapers say, you'll have a very unhappy life." (Interview. Also see the letters from Theodore Roosevelt to Sinclair of April 1906, printed in Upton Sinclair, *My Lifetime in Letters* [Columbia, Mo.: University of Missouri Press, 1960].)

8. Interview.

9. One technique utilized by Sinclair was, if he believed that the press was not carrying the news of some important social upheaval, he would arrange to have himself arrested and, during the arrest or booking, argue the cause to the reporters present.

10. I first presented the ideas in this paragraph in an article titled "Upton Sinclair and the Press: The Brass Check Reconsidered," in *Journalism Quarterly* 49, no. 3 (Autumn 1972):427-36.

11. Upton Sinclair, *Money Writes* (published by the author: Long Beach, Calif., 1927), pp. 124-25.

12. Sinclair told me: "My father had taken to reading Brisbane's column in the *Evening Journal*. He would agree with Brisbane and try to get me to read it. I, wretched little snob, wouldn't have anything to do with it. I had to have five or six years of suffering and struggle before I came to realize that I agreed with Brisbane more than I did with the *Evening Post*." A similar tale appears in the *Autobiography*.

13. *Brass Check*, p. 36.

14. Interview.

15. *Brass Check*, p. 36.

16. *Cup of Fury*, pp. 99-100.

17. Interview.

18. Interview.

19. Upton Sinclair, *Mammonart* (published by the author: Pasadena, Calif., 1924), p. 340.

20. *Brass Check*, pp. 90-92.

21. *Brass Check*, p. 93.

22. *American Outpost*, p. 185.

23. Interview.

24. *Brass Check*, pp. 140-41.

25. *Brass Check*, pp. 94, 254, 255, 338.

26. Interview. Needless to say, Sinclair never was invited to Hearst's "castle," though a number of visitors there stopped off at the Sinclairs' home enroute.

27. *Autobiography*, p. 204.

28. *Brass Check*, pp. 53, 300-301. Sinclair clearly respected Older's judgment. The Fremont Older Papers in the Bancroft Library, University of California, Berkeley, contain a number of letters from Sinclair seeking advice on various topics. See Sinclair to Older, July 6, 1909; Aug. 12, 1910; and Aug. 19, 1929.

29. *Brass Check*, p. 42.

30. *Brass Check*, pp. 42-43.

31. Interview. *Brass Check* contains testimonials from individuals who experienced pressure from advertisers. For example, Frank E. Wolfe, managing editor of the *Los Angeles Herald* (which, at the time, engaged in numerous reform campaigns), wrote an exposé after visiting the site of an aviation meet at a place called Dominguez Hill. He found "abhorrent conditions" at the field. But the meet was sponsored by the local Merchants and Manufacturers Association, which promptly withdrew considerable

advertising. The business manager of the paper "came storming in" to demand a printed apology from Wolfe (pp. 289-90).

32. *Brass Check*, p. 236.

33. *Southern Belle*, p. 221.

34. Sinclair felt very strongly about the evils of alcohol. His books contain many stories of journalists and writers who chose this route of self-destruction. See, for example, *Mammonart* and *Money Writes* and, particularly, *Cup of Fury*, which demonstrated that drinking ruined "one after another of the great . . . men and women whose talents should have been conserved for the benefit of all humanity. . . ." (p. 44).

35. *Autobiography*, p. 101.

36. *Autobiography*, pp. 103-4. Advertising men in New York had told Wilshire that his magazine would be self-sustaining after reaching 400,000 subscribers—thus, the prizes. He reached that figure, but still could not obtain enough advertising.

37. *Autobiography*, pp. 101-4, 149-50.

38. *Autobiography*, p. 108. The version he gave me was, "The chief source of corruption is the businessman who wants some public favor. The city has to take over such enterprises."

39. Interview.

40. Upton Sinclair, *World's End* (New York: Viking Press, 1940), pp. 630-32, 676, 678. A great deal of the material in this first "Lanny Budd" novel was given Sinclair by Steffens. (See the *Autobiography*, p. 294.)

41. Interview. Sinclair used the information given him by Untermyer and Dill in his books *The Metropolis* and *The Money Changers*. He also tapped Mrs. Clarence Mackay and Mrs. Oliver Belmont, whom he met through Brisbane.

42. Interview.

43. Interview.

44. Interview.

45. Interview.

46. Interview.

47. Interview.

48. *Money Writes*, p. 44.

49. *Brass Check*, p. 24.

50. Interview.

51. Interview.

52. *Brass Check*, pp. 29, 31.

53. *Money Writes*, p. 24.

54. *American Outpost*, pp. 206-7.

55. Upton Sinclair, *Letters to Judd* (published by the author: Pasadena, Calif., 1926), p. 28.

56. *Upton Sinclair's Magazine* 1, no. 7 (November 1918):6.

57. *Autobiography*, p. 117.

58. Interview.

59. Upton Sinclair, *The Profits of Religion* (New York: Vanguard Press, 1927; first edition published in 1918), pp. 175-95.

60. Interview.

61. *Autobiography*, pp. 158-60.

62. *Autobiography*, p. 181.

63. See the Harris-Sinclair correspondence in *My Lifetime in Letters*. When Harris sent him a copy of *My Life and Loves*, Sinclair burned it, considering it vile (*My Lifetime*, p. 184).

64. *Mammonart*, p. 353.

65. Interview.

66. In *The Man Who Robbed the Robber Barons* (New York: W. W. Norton, 1965, pp. 198-99), Andy Logan argues that T.R. was thinking of Colonel Mann, editor of *Town Topics*, a New York City weekly, when he spoke of the "muckrake man." He makes a good case. My own impression is that Roosevelt may have had Mann, Sinclair, Lawson, and others in mind, but was primarily concerned with Phillips.

67. *Autobiography,* p. 118.

68. Interview.

69. Interview.

70. *Autobiography*, p. 119.

71. *Money Writes*, p. 25.

72. *Money Writes*, p. 38. In this volume, Sinclair works his way through a long list of former muckrakers and reformers who had compromised themselves. He particularly blames the Curtis publications (George Horace Lorimer, editor of the *Post*) for prostituting writers. "Their stuff is as standardized as soda crackers; originality is taboo, new ideas are treason, social sympathy is a crime, and the one virtue of man is to produce larger and larger quantities of material things" (p. 68).

73. *Brass Check*, p. 336.

74. Interview.

5

PAINTERS OF REFORM: JOHN SLOAN AND ROBERT HENRI

Robert C. Vitz

The explosion in American art circles detonated by the 1908 exhibition of the so-called Ash Can School has long been noted by historians of the Progressive era. The realistic portrayal of New York life that so shocked conservative critics (similar to the literary descriptions by Theodore Dreiser, Stephen Crane, and Ernest Poole), and the readily observed warmth between the artist and the city's seamier side, clearly placed these artists within the bold embrace of the Progressive movement. Yet, while there is much to be said for this surge of urban realism as an expression of social concern, the artists only infrequently perceived of themselves as soldiers in the ranks of reform. Of greater importance and more immediate concern was another battle, which reflected just as clearly, if on a narrower scope, the spirit of the times.

What drew The Eight,* the more accurate label for the Ash Can group, together was neither subject matter nor a shared political philosophy, but a common dislike of academic painting and of the narrow-minded aesthetes who controlled the machinery of exhibitions. Indeed, of the eight painters who exhibited in that historic event at the Macbeth Gallery, Ernest Lawson and William Glackens are more precisely labeled impressionists, Maurice Prendergast was a post-impressionist, while Arthur Davies's idyllic fantasies defy accurate placement. But all found difficulty in

---

*The Eight included Robert Henri, Everett Shinn, William Glackens, Ernest Lawson, George Luks, Arthur Davies, John Sloan, and Maurice Prendergast.

exhibiting their works. As enemies of the genteel tradition, of what passed for sweetness and light, The Eight had expended a great deal of energy in trying to gain acceptance for their various artistic styles. For these eight painters, led by Robert Henri, the slick techniques of academic art denied the strength, the joy, the "real" in American life. Too much emphasis on "beauty" and the "ideal" had led painting into something dishonest and artificial. Their fight, then, was with the sentimental in art and its grip on the art establishment of galleries, museums, critics, and schools. They despised the merely pretty; forthrightness, not elegance, was their theme, and there was no place for the painter of preciousness. In place of technique and formula, The Eight championed a crude, vigorous portrayal of American life, a portrayal that better reflected Whitman's robust optimism than Jacob Riis's disturbing "other half."

Robert Henri was the cement of this rebellion against academic conservatism. An outstanding teacher and painter of considerable reputation, Henri brought both artistic and philosophical direction to those who acknowledged him as their leader. He was a product of the Pennsylvania Academy of Fine Arts and the traditional teachings of Paris, but he drew much of his own artistic style from Thomas Eakins, by way of Thomas Anschutz, and from Franz Hals. American art must consider itself fortunate that Henri returned to his native land in the last year of the nineteenth century, for quite possibly without his spirited guidance and encouragement, George Luks, Everett Shinn, William Glackens, and John Sloan would have remained minor illustrators and newspaper artists in Philadelphia. It was Henri who imbued them with a belief in themselves and a desire to paint the richness of the city around them. "We are not here to do what has already been done," he cautioned, and he encouraged them to seek out their own interests and solutions.[1] He introduced them to the paintings of Manet, Velasquez, and Daumier, to the writings of Whitman and Zola. He widened their intellectual horizons to include Wagner, Dostoevski, and Isadora Duncan.

Henri encouraged them to capture the colorful spectacle of the Bowery, the romance of the docks, and, above all, to observe closely the people who populated the city. "The tramp sits on the edge of the curb," he once said. "He is all huddled up. His body is thick. His underlip hangs. His eyes look fierce. I feel the coarseness of his clothes against his bare legs.... The subject can be as it may, beautiful or ugly. The beauty of a work of art is in the work itself."[2] Boxing and baseball, poker games and beer steins accented the strenuous life that Henri espoused in rebuttal to William Merritt Chase and other academicians. In 1907, it was Henri, as a member of the thirty-man jury for the National Academy of Design's annual show, who exploded when fellow jurors not only rejected paintings by Luks and Sloan but downgraded his own work as well. Withdrawing his two disparaged paintings, he set in motion a train of events that changed American art forever. The immediate outcome was the exhibition of The Eight.

Divisions within the art community were nothing new. In 1882, the American Watercolor Society had witnessed an "insurrection" when numerous artists, disturbed over jury rejections and implied favoritism, instituted a *Salon des Refuses*.[3] In the 1890s, "The Ten," which included John Twachtman and Childe Hassam, had forced recognition for their brand of impressionism. These short-lived rebellions had been preceded some years earlier by the establishment of the Society of American Artists, an offshoot of the National Academy. The Society of American Artists originally stood for more progressive styles, particularly the dark-toned realism of Munich, but in 1907, the society, grown conservative itself, rejoined the National Academy, and academic ranks closed in defense of their own inflated reputations and, in their own minds, the nation's cultural integrity. Drawing its inspiration from similar European academies, and captivated by the warmed-over styles of mid-nineteenth-century French and German art, the National Academy of Design annually displayed repetitions of technical proficiency void of new ideas or even energy. Sentimental genre scenes, romantic landscapes, and allegorical females clad in flowing robes abounded.

Refusing to change their own styles, and yet coveting the public recognition and financial success promised by the letters "N.A." after an artist's name, the Henri crowd found the annual rejections painful and embarrassing. Successfully frozen out of most major exhibitions, their only hope of achieving public recognition lay in circumventing the academy's control of what was recognized as legitimate art. This required an "independent" show and substantial support from journalists. Indeed, to a great extent, the success of The Eight's revolt lay in the growing influence of newspaper art critics. Given this situation, it is unlikely that the National Academy recognized the seriousness of The Eight's revolt, and it was certainly unaware of what artistic pressures would find release through this rebellion.

When The Eight unveiled their canvases at the Macbeth Gallery, they generated more interest in art than had any event since the secession of the Society of American Artists. Conservative critics denounced them as "apostles of ugliness" and the "revolutionary black gang," yet thousands crowded in to view their works. And not all the criticism was negative. Charles Fitzgerald, who was Glackens's brother-in-law, James Gibbons Huneker, Guy Pene du Bois, and Frederick James Gregg wrote almost daily in support of the show, and Mary Fanton Roberts described it as "a phase of national life," "a homegrown art, of our own soil." "Anyone of them will tell you," she declared, "that just now there is no civilization in the world comparable in interest to ours; none so meteoric, so voluble, so turbulent, so unexpected so instinct with life, so swift of change, so full of riotous contrast in light or shade."[4] Vitality and change, individualism and originality—these became the stock phrases used by supportive critics who called into question the current standards of taste. Thus, The Eight were not alone. They represented only the most visible part of an underlying concern with the weariness of academic painting; it was this larger concern and interest that insured the success of the Macbeth show.

The popularity of The Eight's paintings, which led to a year-long traveling exhibition, precluded a repetition the following year, but when 1909 again brought the customary rejections from the major academy shows, Sloan and Henri, joined by Arthur Davies and Walter Kuhn, spearheaded the Exhibition of Independent Artists in 1910. Considerably more ambitious, involving 103 artists and based upon a no jury, no prizes philosophy, the 1910 show directly assaulted the power of the academies, competing directly with the National Academy's spring show. Like its predecessor, the exhibit proved a sensation. "The three floors were crowded to suffocation, absolutely jammed. [A]t 9 o'clock the crowd packed the sidewalk outside waiting to get in. A small squad of police came on the run. It was terrible but wonderful to think that an art show could be so jammed," Sloan exulted in his diary.[5] The crowds, the enthusiasm of supportive critics, the joyous dinner gatherings at Petitpas's (a local restaurant frequented by the painters) helped offset the lack of sales and the personal expenses involved.

In retrospect, one wonders what all the ruckus was about. The urban scenes painted by these realists[6] now appear nostalgic and sentimental, and the obvious mannerisms of Manet, French impressionism, and the muddy colors of the Munich School clearly link them to acceptable art traditions. What apparently so disturbed the academicians was the subject matter and the less than polished style. Or, as George Bellows phrased it: "I think the big impression is that of manliness, frankness, and love of the game. That is always new." Theodore Roosevelt could not have expressed it better.[7]

The challenge to academic art soon drifted out of Henri's control. In 1911, Rockwell Kent, also a Henri student, initiated another "independent" show, but this time it was to include only artists who refused to submit works to the National Academy that year. But this exclusion clause (and perhaps Kent's leadership) ruffled Henri's sense of individualism. He and Sloan, followed by several others, refused to take part. While Kent's show met with only limited success, it revealed the growing turbulence in the art community, and other artists sensed the possibilities of revolt.

Walter Kuhn, Jerome Myers, and Elmer McRae laid the groundwork for the Association of American Painters and Sculptors, and for what ultimately became the Armory Show of 1913. Henri, Sloan, and members of The Eight soon joined that group, but the realists played a decreasingly influential role. By this time, Sloan, emotionally involved with socialism, had turned his energies toward *The Masses*, the socialist magazine, while Henri felt uncomfortable both in a subordinate role and with the new organization's rapidly developing interest in modern, nonrepresentational European art. The real organizers of the Armory Show, Walt Kuhn and Arthur Davies, from the beginning hoped to make the show considerably broader and more liberal than anything previously conceived in the United States. Still, they recognized Henri's influence and potential opposition and sought to circumvent it. Planning to be "the real boss" as secretary, Kuhn wrote his wife, "Of course Henri and the rest will have to be let in, but not until things are chained up so that they can't do any monkey business."[8]

The Armory Show staggered the art world, captured public attention, savagely assaulted academic standards, and hopelessly divided the avant-garde. A year after the show's closing, Henri, followed by the majority of the New York realists, resigned from the Association of American Painters and Sculptors. Always alert to American artistic independence, and not at all in sympathy with the new art spirit emanating from France and Germany, Henri criticized the exhibition for returning the American artist to a colonial position. His symbolic rejection of European modernism substantially reduced the influence of the Henri crowd in the decades to come. Even as casualties of the Armory Show, which was not immediately apparent, however, the New York realists could still claim a bittersweet victory in having initiated a movement that both destroyed the prestige and control of the National Academy and liberalized American art as well.

If the realists paralleled Progressive reformers in their attack on the entrenched forces of artistic conservatism, they also reflected the Progressives' concern for and interest in urban society. The same forces that spawned John Spargo's *The Bitter Cry of the Children*, Robert Hunter's *Poverty*, Upton Sinclair's *The Jungle*, and Stephen Crane's *Maggie* provided an encouraging environment for the artist as well. But Sinclair's Jurgis Rudkus and Crane's Maggie ultimately leave the reader depressed about the urban condition; the New York realists approached the city with humor, sympathy, and understanding. Theodore Dreiser instilled some of that feeling in Eugene Witla, the artist and central character in *The "Genius."* When Witla first arrived in New York fresh from the Midwest, he saw the city as a great spectacle. He constantly walked the streets, enthralled by " the wonder of this thing—the beauty of it. Such seething masses of people! such whirlpools of life!"[9] Dreiser himself "never tired of looking at the hot, hungry, weary slums,"[10] and Eugene Witla is transparently borrowed from the Henri group. Witla's character resembles that of Everett Shinn, while his painting titles have a distinct Sloan ring to them (*Six O'clock*, *After the Theatre*, *East Side Crowd*, and even one of an Italian boy throwing pigeons into the air—Sloan's own *Pigeons* was first exhibited one year before *The "Genius"* was written).

Like Witla, the artists who attached themselves to Henri had started as newspaper artists, an experience that left them with an intimate feeling for the variety of life found amidst the narrow streets and towering buildings. And it was this personal understanding that made them historians of their day. At a time when American art was dominated by the clichés of academicism, the realists sought to convey the energy and vitality of the common person. "Raw reds, raw greens, dirty gray paving stones—such faces! Why this thing fairly shouted its facts," gushed an art critic over one of Witla's canvases. "It seemed to say: I'm dirty, I am commonplace, I am grim, I am shabby, but I am life."[11] The photographer Alfred Stieglitz found much the same inspiration in the poorer neighborhoods. "Nothing charms me so much as walking among the lower classes, studying them carefully, and making mental notes," he told an interviewer. "I dislike the superficial and artificial, and I find less of it among the lower classes."[12] For John Sloan, the "healthy-faced," "solid-legged" children of the slums caught his eye—the slums where "happiness rather than misery in the whole life" made them infinitely more desirable than Fifth Avenue.[13] In Stieglitz's *The Terminal* and *The Steerage*, in Dreiser's Eugene Witla, and in George Bellows's *Steaming Streets* or Sloan's *The Haymarket*, one finds the same keenness of eye and sympathy of mind.

On canvas, then, the New York realists examined without prejudice the swirl of life around them. They viewed the city much as the couple in William Dean Howells's *A Hazard of New Fortunes:*

> It was better than the theater . . . to see those people through their windows: a family party of workfolk at a late tea, some of the men in their shirtsleeves; a woman sewing by a lamp; a mother laying her child in its cradle; a man with his head fallen on his hands upon a table; a girl and her lover leaning over the windowsill together. What suggestion! What drama! What infinite interest![14]

This perpetual theater fascinated the artists. They frequented the crowded beaches, the boxing clubs, the docks, and the dancehalls, and found inspiration for hundreds of paintings and etchings.

Within this group, John Sloan most often prowled the neighborhood around West Fourteenth Street and lower Sixth Avenue. It was Sloan who took most seriously the people who lived there: the ragged children, the Sunday strollers, the regulars at McSorley's Old Ale House, his own friends at Petitpas's. Like Theodore Roosevelt, who once described the Bowery as "one of the great highways of humanity, a highway of seething life, of varied interest, of fun, of work, of sordid and terrible tragedy . . . ,"[15] Sloan felt the human warmth and magnetism of the city. "How necessary it is for an artist of any creative sort to go among *common people*—and not to waste his time among his fellows," he wrote, "for it must be from the other classes . . . that he will get his knowledge of life."[16] As Sloan's diary so often reveals, many of his paintings and etchings came directly from his daily strolls. Once, while on his way to Henri's studio, he saw through a window a hairdresser bleaching a client's hair, attended by a small crowd outside; the result was *Hairdresser's Window.* On another occasion, he observed "a beautiful windstorm, the air full of dust and a sort of panicky terror in all the living things in sight. A broad gray curtain of cloud pushing over the zenith, the streets in wicked misty murk." The next day he began work on *Dust Storm, Fifth Avenue.*[17]

A second vantage point for Sloan's curious eye was the back window of his attic studio on West Twenty-third Street, on the very edge of the turbulent Tenderloin district. From there, he quietly recorded people's lives as observed on roof-top scenes and through bedroom windows: the humor, sadness, and pathos of life. Two girls cleaning their breakfast dishes, he wrote in his diary, their night robes "hanging loose and clinging close to their backs, their gowns are very full of humor of life." Once he observed a baby die in its mother's arms, with the men of the house standing around powerless to prevent the tragedy.[18] *Three A.M., Sunday, Women Drying Their Hair, Pigeons,* and *Backyard, Greenwich Village* all clearly resulted from his window watching. His etchings, particularly the *New York City Life* series, provide the best evidence of his ability to capture the human drama. *Love on the Roof, Roofs, Summer Night, Turning Out the Light,* and *The Woman's Page* all reflect the artist's compassion for his unknown neighbors. "Work, play, love, sorrow, vanity, the schoolgirl, the old mother, the thief, the truant, the harlot. I see them all down there without disguise," he confided to his diary. "These wonderful roofs of New York bring to me all of humanity."[19] For John Sloan, the intimacies of daily life provided a rich source of inspiration: sometimes, quick and casual images, at other times, continuous entertainment that lasted for weeks. In these glimpses of the truth of life, the artist still has much to tell us.

John Sloan, of course, was not alone in his admiration for the city and its people; he merely used the city more effectively. Everett Shinn was one of the first to approach the seamier side of urban life, but both Shinn and William Glackens soon deserted the darker tones of the streets for the bright colors of the entertainment world. George Luks and Robert Henri infrequently strayed into Sloan's world of side street and backyards, and their own sympathy for the lower classes is best revealed in such minor gems as *The Spielers* and *Laughing Child*. George Bellows, a more powerful painter than Sloan, also found the city much to his liking, but only occasionally did he capture the intimacies of the streets. Despite his *Steaming Streets* and *Cliff Dwellers*, Bellows's romance was with the energy of the city rather than with its people.

Perhaps the artist who best paralleled Sloan's view was Jerome Myers. A brother of Gustavus Myers, a muckraking historian of the era, Jerome Myers had turned his back on academicism several years before The Eight had surfaced in New York. Like the Henri circle, Myers rejected technical detail for a more spontaneous method of capturing the moment. He, too, roamed the streets, making quick sketches of people, recording the leisurely moments of life, and he was the only artist to dwell on the importance of music to immigrant life on the Lower East Side. People resting on benches, the dignity of an old Jew enjoying his peace on a summer night, the swirling crowds at a band concert—these are the images left by Myers's brush. And if his work occasionally incorporates the sentimental, he has left, nevertheless, a penetrating record that, at its best, approaches the work of John Sloan.[20]

If the city appeared on canvas and on paper with dignity, there is little to suggest that the artists had anything more than a basic faith in and concern for mankind. This, of course, had been enough for them to earn the epithets of the conservatives. As a group, however, they shunned politics for the most part and engaged in only the most peripheral activity. Yet, on occasion, the New York realists individually tried their hand at painting a more socially conscious message. Shinn's *The Ragpicker*, Eugene Higgins's *Les Pauvres*, and Bellows's *Cliff Dwellers* illustrate the narrow line that separated their aesthetic rebellion from a more explicit political statement. Indeed, *Cliff Dwellers* was originally conceived as an illustration for the socialist magazine *The Masses*, entitled "Why Don't They All Go to the Country for Vacation?" Only in its finished state does the rich vitality of tenement life overshadow the original message.[21] Considering themselves a part of the Bohemian life centered in Greenwich Village (Sloan once defined a Bohemian as "a free man," in contrast to which "the average man is simply a slave."²²), these artists observed, sometimes with enthusiasm, sometimes with skepticism, the political radicalism that dotted the Progressive landscape. Their world embraced Eugene Debs and Morris Hillquit, even Bill Haywood; Van Wyck Brooks and Max Eastman shared their thoughts; and numerous evenings found the artists applauding Isadora Duncan or arguing the merits of Emma Goldman's anarchism.

In this atmosphere of Bohemian radicalism, a radicalism predicated more on being unconventional than on social reform, Robert Henri once again led the way. His emphasis on artistic freedom and individual expression provided the core of his own self-styled philosophical anarchism. "I am not interested in any one school or movement, nor do I care for art as art," he once wrote. "I am interested in the *open forum*, open for every man to come with his word and for every man to come and hear the evidence...."²³ His struggle was for freedom of expression, for open-mindedness, for "investigation in all directions,"²⁴ and he championed many causes. Still, his steadfast devotion to the principle of Emersonian individualism, a sort of laissez-faire of the arts, kept Henri from joining any political organization or movement. He did provide, however, a spirit of justice and truth, of vital democracy, that influenced all who followed him.

Among those painters who followed Henri's lead in the early years of the century, only John Sloan turned his energy directly to political causes. For Sloan, the ethereal anarchism espoused by Henri failed to provide results. Platitudes were no substitute for political action, and increasingly, Sloan felt the need for a personal commitment to reform. "With his demand for the rights of man, and his love of the people...," as Henri once described him,²⁵ Sloan easily slid into the role of political activist. Even his early work had displayed a tendency toward direct comment. *The Coffee Line*, a 1905 dark-toned painting, depicted a line of cold, hungry men waiting for a gratuitous cup of coffee, while such etchings as *Treasure Trove* (a woman scavenging in a waste barrel) and *Fifth Avenue Critics* (the ostentatious snobbery of the carriage trade) reveal a sharp bite.

Still, Sloan consciously tried to separate his developing political views from his development as a painter, reserving his strongest statements for cartoons and illustrations. He never felt comfortable as a propagandist, and even his activity as a member of the Socialist party sometimes amazed him. To him, if a painting expressed a definite political message, as opposed to satire, it lost its claim as art. He preferred to follow the path of Hogarth and Daumier rather than to become a political cartoonist. "I am rather more interested in the human beings themselves than in the schemes for betterment," he wrote in 1909. "In fact, I rather wonder if they will be so interesting when they are all comfortable and happy."[26] Ironically, as Sloan recorded that thought he was already moving swiftly toward active socialism.

The defeat of William Jennings Bryan in 1908, coupled with the news that several labor unions had supported Taft, dismayed the somewhat naive Sloan. A month later, the art critic Charles Wisner Barrell found Sloan a receptive listener to his views on socialism.[27] Sloan's diary, which he kept faithfully from 1906 to 1913, charts his growing involvement with the Socialist party. On Christmas Day in 1908, he noted with pleasure that Thomas Anschutz, his much-admired teacher at the Pennsylvania Academy of Fine Arts, had endorsed the socialist cause. The following spring, although he balked at admitting an obvious socialist message into this work, he referred to the Socialist party as "the proper party." During the course of the next year, his political reading embraced Oscar Wilde's *The Soul of Man Under Socialism*, Whitman's "Song of Myself," and the Socialist party platform of 1908. "Can't understand why the workers of the country were so disinterested or intimidated as not to vote en masse for these principles," he commented after reading the platform.

Comments on the injustices of the night court, the sometimes cruel behavior of policemen, the human destructiveness of American society, and the need for workers to organize sprinkle his daily entries. On Memorial Day in 1909, he watched the wagon loads of children being driven out to the park. "Reminded me of loads of cattle going to slaughter houses. Very beautiful they were, in light colored dressed, packed together—like flower beds of youth and beauty—but, ultimately, for the slaughter."[28] By August, Sloan had started contributing cartoons free to the socialist newspaper *The Call*, and in September, when encouraged to vote Democratic by an election officer, he responded, "No thanks, Socialist or nothing."[29]

As Sloan drew closer to socialism, a bitter tone crept into his diary. A parade of school children, which earlier might have symbolized joy and hope, now left him saddened: "This youth and happiness so soon to be worn away by contact with the social conditions, the grind and struggle for existence." He pointedly noted the "murder" of the Spanish anarchist Francesco Ferrer, and his cartoons became increasingly more strident. Although, at the end of 1909, he felt he had passed "the feverish state" and felt "more quiet" and "happier minded," socialism continued to dominate his activities. His reading expanded to include George Bernard Shaw's *An Unsocial Socialist*, Maxim Gorky's *Three of Us*, Jack London's *Martin Eden*, two socialist magazines, and several unspecified books by Arthur Morrison, probably fictional accounts of London's East End slum life.[30] He expressed his opposition to churches by refusing to attend services on Christmas Day, and in March 1910, the Philadelphia general strike made him "proud" that his old city was "cradling the newer greater Liberty for America!" At the same time, he and his wife, Dolly, joined Branch One of the Socialist party.[31] In May, he ruefully commented that few of his friends found socialism attractive, but lagging friendships did not deter his activism. He enthusiastically supported the myriad party activities, passed out pamphlets, marched on behalf of the Lawrence, Massachusetts, strikers, and twice ran for state office as a Socialist. Sloan's anger had found an outlet.[32]

When George R. Kirkpatrick approached him about illustrating his book *War—What for?*, Sloan jumped at the chance to explain to the workers "that capital and the shopkeepers make use of them against each other in warfare." The Triangle Shirtwaist Company factory fire of 1911, in which 145 girls died (Sloan condemned it as "a sort of holocaustic celebration in honor of the fact that the Supreme Court of N.Y. yesterday declared the Employer's Liability Act of the last season unconstitutional."), elicited a pungent cartoon from the artist: "A black triangle, each side marked ('Rents,' 'Interest,' 'Profit') death on one side, a fat capitalist on the other, and a charred body of a girl in the center."[33] This type of cartoon, which he did for such socialist publications as *The Coming Nation*, *The Call*, and *Appeal to Reason*, provided Sloan with an outlet for his most bitter indictments of American society. But this obvious propaganda, however beneficial as an emotional release, clashed with his own definition of art. The appearance of *The Masses* resolved his dilemma.

Founded by the Socialist Piet Vlag, *The Masses* provided a unique and, for a time, more comfortable outlet for Sloan's developing political concerns. This remarkable magazine, under Max Eastman's capable editorship, consciously sought to merge art and politics in an appeal to all elements on the radical Left, but it held a particular fascination for the Bohemian intellectual. Its latitudinarian views and its emphasis on satirical art, in part an influence from the German magazines *Simplicissimus* and *Jugend*, appealed to Sloan, and both he and Dolly plunged feverishly into making it a success. Eastman fondly recalled that Sloan "loved *The Masses* and would waste time on it in the same childish way I would."[34] Sloan's cartoons and occasional articles were offered free (as were those of most contributors), and the two years before the outbreak of World War I found him devoting less attention to painting. With Sloan as art editor, George Bellows, Rockwell Kent, and Stuart Davis also became regular contributors, and the drawings and cartoons published in *The Masses* provided a fresh and penetrating appraisal of the nation's social ills.

Although Sloan rarely provided a strong political statement in his work for *The Masses*, if a situation fired his anger, he could equal the sharp-edged indignation of Art Young or Robert Minor, cartoonists on the magazine, as he did in his cover on the Ludlow, Colorado, strike. Here, he drew a striking miner, with revolver, holding a dead child in his arms, while at his feet lie his dead wife and baby. More typical for Sloan, however, was *The Unemployed*, which presented a well-to-do couple enjoying an evening in a private box at the theater.[35] In the years of Sloan's influence on the magazine, much of the illustrative work reflected a sympathetic portrayal of the people, tinged with social satire—a far more comfortable artistic style for the artist than were the more blatant comments he had sent to *The Call*.

John Sloan was not a doctrinaire Socialist, nor was he particularly well read on socialist theory. He came to socialism in search of individual freedom, and from a rejection of the existing political arrangement. In his diary, he defined socialism as "the helping [of] the whole human race to reach that mental advance necessary to abolish most human ills."[36] His criticisms of American society did not call for an overthrow of the system. He saw change in terms of reform rather than revolution, and the more radical socialist dogma seems not to have influenced him. For Sloan, evil was not found in theory, but in everyday existence; his enemies were not so much capitalists and warlords, but petty officials and policemen. Nothing triggered his indignation more quickly than human meanness—a policeman beating a drunk or the treatment meted out to the victims of New York's night court. Yet human kindness, not violence, lay at the core of his politics. He disagreed with Bill Haywood (although after the successful Lawrence strike, he became temporarily more supportive of the tactics of the Industrial Workers of the World [IWW] and found himself drawn to the humanism of Eugene Debs ("one of the most Christ-like men I have ever met").[37]

This sympathy for mankind eventually brought Sloan into conflict with the more strident voices on *The Masses*. In reaction to a new political propaganda ushered in by the tensions of the war in Europe, he came down forcefully on the side of artistic integrity. For several months, a quarrel raged over the placement of political captions under Sloan's illustrations, and finally, in 1916, he resigned from the staff, followed by Kent, Bellows, Davis, and Glenn O. Coleman. As cartoonist Art Young somewhat contemptuously described it, the artists wanted "to run pictures of ash cans and girls hitching their skirts up on Horatio Street—regardless of ideas —and without title."[38] Beneath this confrontation between social satire and social propaganda lay a more serious question for Sloan. Despite his own personal socialist vision, his early enthusiasm for the Socialist party waned after several years, perhaps a casualty of his skepticism of all institutions. The outbreak of war in 1914 had left him discouraged over the failure of socialism to defy the blare of the bugle, and about the time he left *The Masses*, he allowed his Socialist party membership to lapse. Furthermore, stimulated by the Armory Show, his painting took on a new look, leaving the somber realism of the city behind. Although he remained sensitive to both socialism and the currents of urban life, Sloan's role as a Progressive painter had ended.

John Sloan's social activism separated him from the other New York realists only by degree; with perhaps the exception of Everett Shinn, all shared his concern for social issues. Robert Henri's professed anarchism—an abstract creed based upon human perfectibility and individual freedom—had encouraged all who followed him to question institutions and social restraints. Henri admired and espoused the views of Emma Goldman, became a devotee of Isadora Duncan's expressive dance (as did Sloan), but his emphasis on an unfettered individualism, in the tradition of Thoreau and Whitman, checked any personal involvement in organized movements. However, he did contribute several illustrations to *The Masses* and, in 1912, accepted Emma Goldman's invitation to teach evening art classes at the Ferrer School.[39] George Luks, William Glackens, and Arthur Davies also contributed occasionally to *The Masses*, largely due to their friendship with Sloan, while Stuart Davis, Rockwell Kent, Glenn Coleman, and George Bellows became regular contributors to the radical journal. None shared Sloan's political intensity, and when Sloan left *The Masses*, they, too, drifted away from social statements.

By 1916, then, the artistic flowering that had found nourishment in the soil of the city had withered. Reflecting the decline of Progressive reform, and esthetically challenged by the outburst of modernism at the Armory Show, the New York realists explored other styles and other themes. Sloan turned to landscapes and nudes and a brightened palette, Glackens continued along the path of Renoir, while Bellows searched for inspiration on the Maine coast. Henri spent more and more time away from the city, finding New Mexico, Spain, and Ireland now more suited to his temperament. The city itself had changed as well: neighborhoods lost their charm, intimate restaurants and old haunts disappeared, and soaring skyscrapers obscured the human drama. What needed saying in 1900 no longer required saying. The realists had made their statement.

How, then, does one assess the place of Henri, Sloan, and their fellow realists? Certainly, their politics seem tame and naive today. Although they talked about anarchism and socialism, admired Isadora Duncan, and supported many of the radical causes of their day, neither Village Boheminanism nor radical politics held more than superficial attraction for them. They were predominantly middle class in background, and their political views harbored Progressive ideals. Those issues that most concerned Progressive reformers—distribution of wealth, expanding capitalism, and political integrity—concerned the New York realists as well, but they viewed the issues from the perspective of the common man, not from social theory. Their paintings revealed them, not so much socialists as Jeffersonian democrats.

If their politics have, on occasion, been distorted, so, too, has their painting. In retrospect, their work is conservative and more clearly identified with the nineteenth century than with the twentieth. There is little to be found in their canvases that suggests any of the major trends in art that developed after the Armory Show; nevertheless, they did provide a distinct contrast with the realism that preceded them. Realism was expected to be popular and uplifting, not socially instructive. Rustic harmony and sentimental genre paintings prevailed, and the New York realists' scenes of common people pursuing common tasks, set in an urban locale, did not conform to the accepted notions of the ideal. Consequently, even the mild "message" implied in their work offended the guardians of tradition. Still, too much has been made of the "Ash Can" label. If the Henri crowd painted shabby neighborhoods and street urchins, they also painted parks and theaters and Fifth Avenue carriages. Their eye was eclectic, and their canvases were personal statements about the city, not just the slums. Beauty was not defined by neighborhood.

What set the New York realists apart was neither their painting nor their politics, it was their liberating philosophy of art that earned them lasting importance. In their willingness to explore new themes, to paint for personal expression rather than for polished technique, and, above all, to challenge the rigid control of the National Academy, they provided a Progressive spirit that helped transform American art. They sought to join art to life, to remove it from the province of curators and aesthetes and the stuffy corridors of the academies. "In America, or any other country, art will not be attained by the possession of canvases in palatial museums, by the purchase and bodily owning of art," lectured Henri. "The greatness can only come by the art spirit entering into the very life of the people...."[40]

Henri's "art spirit" called for a democracy in art and an unfettering of human individualism. One can scarcely envision the Armory Show without the Henri storm that preceded it, or the course of American art in this century without recognizing the influence of Henri and Sloan as teachers. From their classes poured forth dozens of talented artists who furthered the development of America's art. Many were realists, such as Edward Hopper, Reginald Marsh, and Aaron Bohrod, but others, like Niles Spencer, Man Ray, and George L. K. Morris, explored the paths of abstraction. Despite the fact that neither Henri nor Sloan felt comfortable with the new currents in art, they continued to preach a liberating philosophy. Their real message to America was that art could not be proscribed by academic theory. All life was art.

NOTES

1. Robert Henri, *The Art Spirit* (Philadelphia: J. B. Lippincott Co., 1951), p. 2.

2. Quoted in *American Painting, 1900-1917*, by the editors of Time-Life Books (New York: Time-Life Books, 1970), p. 15.

3. Kathleen A. Foster, "The Watercolor Scandal of 1882: An American Salon des Refuses," *Archives of American Art Journal* 19, no. 2 (1979).

4. Giles Edgarton [Mary Fanton Roberts], "The Younger American Painters: Are They Creating a National Art?" *Craftsman* 13 (February 1908):524.

5. John Sloan, *John Sloan's New York Scene*, ed. Bruce St. John and with an introduction by Helen Farr Sloan (New York: Harper and Row, 1965), Apr. 1, 1910, pp. 405-6.

6. The New York realists included Henri, Sloan, Glackens, Luks, and Shinn from The Eight, as well as George Bellows, Jerome Myers, Glenn O. Coleman, Rockwell Kent, and several lesser-known artists.

7. George Bellows to Joe Taylor, ca. April 1910, quoted in Charles H. Morgan, *George Bellows, Painter of America* (New York: Reynal and Co., 1965), p. 110.

8. Garnett McCoy, "An Archivist's Choice: Ten of the Best," *Archives of American Art Journal* 19, no. 2 (1979):14.

9. Theodore Dreiser, *The "Genius"* (New York: World Publishing Co., 1915), p. 108.

10. Theodore Dreiser, *A Book About Myself* (New York: Boni and Liveright, 1922), p. 210.

11. Dreiser, *The "Genius,"* p. 231.

12. William Innes Homer, *Alfred Stieglitz and the American Avant-Garde* (Boston: New York Graphic Society, 1977), p. 16.

13. Sloan, *New York Scene*, Feb. 13, 1906, p. 13.

14. William Dean Howells, *A Hazard of New Fortunes* (New York: Signet Classic, 1965), p. 66.

15. Quoted in Van Wyck Brooks, *John Sloan, A Painter's Life* (New York: E. P. Dutton and Co., 1955), p. 55.

16. Ibid., p. 49.

17. Sloan, *New York Scene*, June 10, 1906, p. 40, and June 5, 1907, p. 133.

18. Ibid., June 11, 1906, p. 40, and June 23, 1906, p. 43.

19. Mary Fanton Roberts, "John Sloan: His Art and His Inspiration," *Touchstone* 4 (February 1919):362.

20. Grant Holcomb, "The Forgotten Legacy of Jerome Myers (1867-1940): Painter of New York's Lower East Side," *The American Art Journal* 9 (May 1977):78-91.

21. Morgan, *George Bellows*, p. 170.

22. Joseph J. Kwiat, "John Sloan: An American Artist as Social Critic, 1900-1917," *Arizona Quarterly* 10 (Spring 1954): 61-62.

23. Henri, *The Art Spirit*, p. 169.

24. Quoted in Milton W. Brown, *American Painting, From the Armory Show to the Depression* (Princeton: Princeton University Press, 1955), p. 10.

25. Robert Henri, "The New York Exhibition of Independent Artists," *Craftsman* 18 (May 1910):162.

26. Sloan, *New York Scene*, Apr. 15, 1909, p. 306.

27. Ibid., Nov. 6, 1908, p. 260, and Dec. 7, 1908, p. 268.

28. Ibid., Dec. 25, 1908, p. 273; May 5, 1909, p. 310; May 21, 1909, p. 313; May 26, 1909, p. 314; May 31, 1909, p. 315; June 9, 1909, p. 317; and June 12, 1909, p. 318.

29. Ibid., Aug. 16, 1909, p. 328, and Sept. 21, 1909, pp. 335-36.

30. Ibid., Oct. 2, 1909, p. 338; Oct. 15, 1909, p. 342; Dec. 19, 1909, p. 361; Jan. 20, 1910, p. 377; and Jan. 29, 1910, p. 380.

31. Ibid., Dec. 25, 1909, p. 364; Mar. 6, 1910, pp. 383-94; and Feb. 1, 1910, p. 381.

32. Ibid., May 16, 1910, p. 422, and Feb. 2, 1911, pp. 600-601.

33. Ibid., June 13, 1910, p. 433; Mar. 25, 1911, p. 520; and Mar. 26, 1911, p. 520.

34. Quoted in Richard Fitzgerald, *Art and Politics: Cartoonists of the "Masses" and "Liberator"* (Westport, Conn.: Greenwood Press, 1973), p. 131.

35. These cover illustrations are found in the issues of March 1913 and June 1914.

36. Sloan, *New York Scene*, May 14, 1911, p. 536.

37. Ibid., see parenthetical comment on p. 382.

38. David Scott, *John Sloan* (New York: Watson-Guptill Publications, 1975), p. 114. See also Fitzgerald, *Art and Politics*, pp. 27-28.

39. William Innes Homer, *Robert Henri and His Circle* (Ithaca, N.Y.: Cornell University Press, 1969), pp. 173-74.

40. Henri, *The Art Spirit*, p. 190.

6

RESPONSE TO REFORM: CONSERVATIVES AND THE PROGRESSIVE ERA

Edwina C. Smith

Just as there were many kinds of Progressives, so, too, were there many types of conservatives. Conservatives of the Gilded Age approached the Progressive era in different ways. As Gerald McFarland has shown, some of the old moralistic mugwumps adapted their ideas to the new age and became Progressive urban reformers.[1] Meanwhile, others found the new trends unacceptable, and they opposed Progressive reforms.[2] Conservative politicians, on the whole, were more predictable. Like Nelson Aldrich, Rhode Island's powerful senator, they continued in the Progressive period the battles they had fought against various reforms during the Gilded Age. A few, however, while still conservative, had reform ideas of their own.

In the early administration of Theodore Roosevelt, two senators, in particular, spoke for principled political conservatism. George F. Hoar of Massachusetts and Orville H. Platt of Connecticut served together in the United States Senate for a quarter of a century.[3] They shared much in common as old-line Republicans, yet each made a different adjustment to the changes and challenges of the Progressive era. Never close friends—indeed, at times bitterly at odds with each other—Platt and Hoar played very different roles in the Senate by 1900. Platt was a member of the Senate's inner circle of power, the "Big Four." Hoar was on the periphery of power, still respected for his long and distinguished service but, after his battle against imperialism, increasingly out of touch with the ruling clique.

The careers of both men spanned three eras of Republican and national history. They began their public lives as antislavery Republicans. During the late nineteenth century, they shared their party's goals of encouraging economic development and of promoting national welfare and unity through government action. For these purposes, both remained devoted to the principle of tariff protection to the end of their lives. Finally, in the Progressive era, they struggled, sometimes in opposition, with the problems of large-scale industry, labor conflict, and the consequences of American foreign expansion.

Both men shared a common heritage that influenced their careers as politicians and conservatives. Each grew up in a family dedicated to the abolitionist cause. The Platt home was a station on the underground railway, and the senator's parents were members of a much-harassed abolitionist group in the hamlet of Judea, Connecticut.[4] Both of Hoar's parents ran afoul of the authorities in their attempts to aid blacks, northern and southern. In the 1840s and 1850s, young Hoar joined his father in the Free-Soil movement. The ideals of the antislavery cause never left him.[5]

With such backgrounds, it is not surprising that Hoar and Platt maintained a concern with black rights and a hostility to racist policies for the rest of their lives. Old-line Republicans such as these, not the Progressives, spoke most often in defense of blacks during the Progressive era.[6] Both men had supported federal aid for black education in the 1880s and had condemned the 1890 sacrifice of the Federal Elections Bill for a tariff, although each was an ardent protectionist.[7] Hoar opposed imperialism, in part, because he feared it would retard black progress at home, and he voiced dismay at the racism of American soldiers in the Philippines. He still hoped for eventual equality of the races but could not be too optimistic. After all, he wrote sadly, Americans were now a nation "intent upon crushing a people who were aspiring to liberty in the Far East."[8]

Platt had a lifelong interest in black history and, in 1903, scorned the racist persecution of a black postmistress in Indianola, Mississippi. Roosevelt's refusal to dismiss her received his vigorous support. Hoar lectured his southern friends for their criticism of the president's appointment of a black customs collector of Charleston, South Carolina. Roosevelt, he told them, swore to uphold the Constitution and because he occupied "a house belonging to the whole people," could not "exclude any part of the people from constitutional rights or equality under the law, or from social courtesies, merely by reason of race."[9] Hoar personally disliked racism. In the next world, he once observed, "they invite colored men to dinner." His feelings about "the rights of men without regard to their color," he noted in 1903, had estranged him even from his own party.[10]

Both men exhibited a very moralistic approach to political issues, in part, a reflection of their early Republican heritage. They repeatedly emphasized principles and moral questions of right and wrong on a variety of issues. Each judged the conduct of corporations and nations by the same moral principles as that of individuals. This attitude distinguished them from those Progressives who emphasized reform of the economic *system* rather than individual responsibility.[11]

On the matter of corporate regulation, Platt endorsed the individual moral viewpoint. "A corporation should be treated as an individual," he said. "If it behaves itself it should be respected; if it undertakes to do wrong it should be restrained." A well-conducted corporation was a benefit to the country, but if it "goes into unfair dealings, inequitable doings, then it is a disgrace and a shame. But that is true of the individual just as it is of the corporation." And he once asked the great meatpacker, Gustavus Swift, whether special favors to large shippers were "quite the right thing as between man and man."[12]

Hoar felt much the same way. In explaining his antitrust bill in 1903, which would make *individuals* liable for corporate abuses, he emphasized that wrongful conduct, not large size, was his target and that the real danger was industrial combinations. As he observed privately, "Our managers of the vast corporations, I am sorry to say, have got to regard the public as a flock of sheep to be sheared, or a drove of swine to have their throats cut." Morality and ethics applied to the nation as well. Hoar said to Roosevelt, in the wake of the Panama Revolution of 1903: "I hope I shall not live, Mr. President, to the time when if the country is to do anything in which I am concerned, my first thought will not be her honor, and only the second thought for her interest."[13]

The amoral tenets of Social Darwinism held no appeal for either senator. As to the "bugbear of so-called free competition" and its corollary, "survival of the fittest," Platt stated in 1887, during debate on the Interstate Commerce Act, "I deny and repudiate them both. There is a competition which is not lawful . . . which is not honest. . . . If by 'competition and survival of the fittest' is meant competition and destruction of the weakest, I say it is anti-Christian; it is anti-republican," and would "lapse us into barbarism." It was nothing but the "old despotic idea that 'might makes right,'" that "men are ruled by the strong hand, and not by regard for the moral law."[14] Such an attitude contrasted markedly with that of Platt's colleague and conservative of a different stripe, Nelson Aldrich, a man who valued power for its own sake and who believed in the survival of the strong.[15]

Hoar and Platt were of the generation that first had to come to grips with the impact of modern industrialism. Late in life, both would look back to a time of simpler ways of doing business, of more intimate relations between employer and worker, a time when the individual seemed to have more chance of success. This loss of individual opportunity haunted each senator as he struggled with the problems of monopoly and industrial combinations. Part of their willingness to accept some government regulation came from their desire to preserve chances for ordinary men. As Platt wrote in 1894, the dwindling opportunity for a man to build his own business in a world of huge industrial combinations "is one of the things in this country that may well engage the profoundest thought of the political economist."[16]

In the growth of monopoly capitalism (and in the Socialist's answer to it), Hoar saw the destruction of individual worth, ambition, and achievement. These trends meant that local industries and individual workers alike would be submitting to an impersonal central power that made no distinction between excellence and mediocrity. With no difference recognized between "the energetic and the slothful," the intelligent and the incompetent, "the great principle of emulation and individual excellence" would be destroyed. A man's personal merit would have no significance. To Hoar, such a result destroyed "everything which makes life worth living or manhood worth respecting." And so he tried to find a way to curb monopoly power, without going to the extreme of complete government control.[17]

Despite their political and philosophical similarities, their individual dealings with President Theodore Roosevelt were quite different. Platt quickly formed both an easy, informal friendship and a sound working relationship with Roosevelt. They consulted frequently on issues and shared a love of the outdoors. During the 1904 campaign, the Connecticut senator worked hard for Roosevelt's nomination and election, defending him against his many critics, and he advised him on the conduct of the campaign. The two men, at times, disagreed on policies, and Platt sometimes found the bumptious president's ways upsetting; nonetheless, their working relationship was satisfying to both and helped to smooth relations between the executive branch and the Senate.[18]

Hoar, in contrast, never became close to Roosevelt, personally or politically. The *Boston Evening Transcript* could not resist noting that Hoar was the only Massachusetts legislator to find anything to criticize in the new president's first message to Congress.[19] In good part, the estrangement grew out of Hoar's unstinting opposition to American imperialism in the Philippines. Criticizing the war itself, speaking up for the rights of the Filipino patriot Mabini, and pushing for a congressional investigation of American military conduct, he was a perpetual aggravation to Roosevelt. His criticism of the president's actions in the Panama affair further alienated the two men.[20] He disagreed with Roosevelt more frequently, he noted in 1903, "than with any other Republican President since we had Republican Presidents, with the exception of President Arthur." Hoar thought Roosevelt courageous and sincere, if a bit impulsive, but too inclined to defer to his official advisors. At any rate, he commented somewhat sadly, he was not in the president's confidence. While Roosevelt always treated him with kindness when they met, "He does not consult me much, even about important matters in my own State."[21]

During the early 1900s, the closing years of their careers, Hoar and Platt served together on the Senate Judiciary Committee, with Hoar as chairman (Platt succeeded him on his death, in late 1904). Here, the two men confronted the problems of regulation of industry and legislation dealing with the rights of labor in the Progressive era. Often they did not agree. In fact, from a personal point of view, things started off badly. After Hoar's death, Platt related that he had been offered a place on the committee in the 1880s but had deferred to Hoar's wish to have the spot. Had he taken it then, Platt would have become chairman instead of Hoar. Platt felt that the latter had never shown any appreciation for his sacrifice. Yet Platt was not one to bear a grudge, in part, because he was not personally an ambitious man. And so he could say during Hoar's last illness: "While I have had some pretty close hugs from him, I feel very kindly toward him and realize that he has been one of the remarkable men in our history."[22]

In spite of their specific disagreements on policies, the two senators shared a common conception of their roles as conservatives in an age of reform. In the vast economic changes of their time, both feared a threat of tremendous social upheaval, even revolution, that would undermine or destroy the political society they cherished. Although to a different degree, each was willing to expand the role of the central government to ward off such revolutionary change. In this sense, as in their support of government action to promote economic growth, they can be called centralizing conservatives, in contrast to those who opposed any increase in the government's role in the economy. The *limits* they set on acceptable change separated them from the Progressive reformers.[23]

Hoar and Platt expressed their common fear of social and political upheaval many times. Platt sensed the danger well before the bad years of the 1890s. In arguing, during the 1880s, for the right of the federal government to regulate the railroads, he warned a rigid laissez-faire merchant: "Did it ever occur to you that when business makes its own laws, and the people cannot stand them, the people will destroy the government?" Much of the prevailing discontent in the country, he wrote privately in 1892, had "its foundation in the conduct of the capitalistic classes." Thus, while he vacillated a good deal on trust control, largely because of a fear of overreacting to unreasoning public sentiment, Platt did think some action had to be taken. After the Sherman Antitrust Act of 1890, he tended to shun further legislation but advocated pursuit of individual trusts. In 1904, he felt that "the beef trust ought to be pursued" and that "the tobacco trust needs a little anti-trust medicine." And the then current attacks on Standard Oil, he commented shortly before his death, would perhaps "be a good thing for it."[24]

The 1902 anthracite coal strike severely disturbed the Connecticut senator, and he applauded Roosevelt's success in settling it. On this he differed from his Massachusetts colleague. Hoar could not approve a threat to have the government seize private property. Such action, he felt, was unconstitutional and would constitute state socialism. For Platt, however the need to preserve the social order against potential revolution outweighed any such considerations. He undertook a personal campaign to convince a number of wealthy businessmen, angered over Roosevelt's action, of their folly. In their criticism of the president, he pointed out, these people had forgotten "what was apparent to all careful and thoughtful observers at the time, namely: that if the strike had continued for a fortnight longer, there was a serious danger of riot, bloodshed, and indeed, possible revolution." Hungry and cold men were dangerous, he warned. "I regard that as the most critical period in our history since the War," and had Roosevelt not ended the strike, "there would have developed a condition of affairs that no man could have forseen the end of."[25]

Hoar also responded to the revolutionary dangers he perceived, but in a more concrete way, at least during the Roosevelt years. On December 17, 1902, "to the surprise of all his colleagues," he announced his intention of introducing a new bill for the regulation of trusts and corporations engaged in interstate commerce. According to the *Boston Evening Transcript*, no one had known of Hoar's plans. A main author of the old Sherman Act, he was ready to take an additional step now that the earlier legislation had been tested in the courts.[26]

While Hoar was preparing his bill, he warned the president of Clark University that he would soon have to say something on trusts and great capital accumulations "which will be exceedingly displeasing to Mr. Rockefeller and Mr. Carnegie." He felt that he had to "call attention pretty emphatically to the great danger to the Republic from these vast unchecked fortunes." After the introduction of his completed bill, and having received some criticism of it, Hoar defended its necessity to one hostile businessman. It was "barely possible," he wrote, "that there are signs of an impending revolution, a revolution likely to be not merely political and social, but likely, if it occur, to throw all our business and social order into confusion, which are apparent to me, but which are not apparent to you." While no alarmist, Hoar did think it time for conservative change, time "to deal with these questions slowly, deliberately, and carefully."[27]

Hoar's bill was hardly radical. His concern was the tremendous power of huge capital accumulations, and he was proposing ways to prevent the corruption of the national economic and political fabric. His proposal defined the terms under which corporations could engage in interstate commerce: submission of corporate financial returns; prohibition of watered stock and of stock purchases except for cash; prohibition of oppression of rivals or the public; and, most important, personal liability of corporate officers and members for violations of the law. Hoar had no doubts about the power of Congress to pass such a law. Under its constitutional duty to regulate commerce, Congress had the right "to prohibit all transactions of Interstate or International commerce by corporations," artificial beings created by the state. "We have the right to impose on them any condition that may be thought fit."[28]

Unfortunately, most of Hoar's colleagues on the Judiciary Committee, including Platt, as well as the Senate Republican leadership, agreed neither on the constitutionality nor on the desirability of his proposed bill. It died in committee in 1903.[29]

As conservatives, Hoar and Platt set certain limits on the kind and extent of changes they would accept in government control of American life and the economy. A basic premise they both shared was the importance of preserving national industrial growth and progress. For them, here was the dilemma of modern industrialism: they feared its abuses, but it was also one of the great achievements of modern America and essential to her survival. As Platt said: "The development . . . of the industries of a country" brought it "greatness and power and glory." Large-scale business, with vast capital at its disposal, he contended, was a necessity of the age and if conducted "honestly and fairly," a "blessing." No proper reform should cripple industrial progress. Platt could not support the Littlefield Antitrust Bill of 1903 (a measure similar to Hoar's), he announced, because of provisions that were "mischievous and would work great injury to the business of the United States."[30]

Hoar tried to find a middle ground between curbing corporate dangers and perserving the nation's industrial strength, which was the essence of his antitrust bill. His speech explaining it interspersed warnings of the perils of uncontrolled corporate power with statements about the need for great industries. "They are necessary to national greatness," he proclaimed. "We cannot maintain our equality among the nations of the earth and we cannot achieve the supremacy now easily within our grasp without them." In protecting ourselves, we must take care not to "destroy them or cramp them." He hoped, through his bill, to "give them a law which will not impair their strength and not check their natural and rightful growth."[31]

The second major deterrent to reform for these men, especially Platt, was their hostility to what they considered to be the indiscriminate attacks on wealth and property that were characteristic of their times. The Connecticut senator regarded the 1894 income tax proposal as an integral part of this assault, and he fought it as such. There appeared to be, he asserted, "a prevailing idea that because some people acquire fortunes improperly, therefore the cry should be raised, 'Down with every man who owns anything.'" All past ideas about the legitimate acquisition of property were to be discarded, and anyone with money was to be "mulcted in some way and his property taken away from him." This kind of idea offended Platt's basic beliefs—his conservatism and his devotion to the republican form of government. "The right of property lies at the foundation of government," he declared. That right was "as sacred as the rights of life and liberty, and . . . no country which has not a just regard for the rights of private property can go on progressively as a republic."[32]

Similar feelings about popular prejudice caused Platt to resist more trust legislation during the Roosevelt years. "There seems to be a perfect craze now regarding the operations of those concerns called 'trusts' particularly the prominent ones," he wrote in 1905. The behavior of the Kansas legislature was bad enough, but even worse, Congress itself was "just as likely to go wild some day . . . and a conservative man liable at any moment to find himself trampled out of sight."[33]

Hoar shared this concern over precipitate, potentially damaging actions but was more flexible in his response. On the trust issue, he noted in connection with his own bill, the "important question" was "whether the American people can control their impatience so as to deal with this great question carefully, and await a remedy which it may take some years to mature and perfect."[34] He was not opposed to all actions but only favored cautious methods.

Both senators also were reluctant to act because of their perception of the Constitution and their dislike of government "paternalism." They insisted on strict constitutionality for any proposed legislation, even if they disagreed on what constituted it. In 1890, Platt criticized the Sherman Antitrust Act on constitutional grounds. When asked by a colleague what the harm was in passing unconstitutional bills since the courts could review them later, he replied tersely: "Whenever Congress passes a bill which the concurrent sentiment of Congress believes to be unconstitutional it does greater damage to the people of this country than is well to be calculated." Platt's early objections to various antitrust bills were also based, in part, on his doubts about their constitutionality, particularly in light of the then recent Supreme Court decisions. Hoar, however, had no qualms about the constitutionality of his own bill, and he defended it on that basis.[35]

In criticizing legislation, Platt spoke frequently of the danger of government "paternalism." By that he meant the assumption by government of the individual's rightful responsibility for his own welfare. For him, this often marked the difference between proper and improper government activity. The latter could not do a great deal about "capitalistic abuses," he wrote in 1892, "unless we . . . change the whole character of our Government into paternalism which would be worse." Although the government had the right to regulate railroads, to give it power to *fix* rates would open the way to "paternalistic government." And so, Platt fought the Townsend Rate Bill during 1904-1905, a measure he considered a reflection of the rate-making "craze" that seemed to have taken possession of the country. While willing to pass "proper and desirable legislation" to remedy abuses, he did not want "to do foolish and indiscrete things." He felt the same about individual welfare. The government could provide jobs *indirectly* through a national policy such as the protective tariff, but it could not directly relieve unemployment. That was paternalism and "class legislation."[36]

The two senators had some of their sharpest conflicts, during the Progressive era, over legislation to protect the rights of labor. Actually, they agreed closely on the *theoretical* rights of labor, and both abhorred violence in labor conflicts. The disputes arose over protecting these rights in *practice*. Workers had the right to organize in unions, they allowed, just as capital could combine in corporations. In fact, as Hoar pointed out, organization was essential if workers were to bargain on an equal basis with large corporations for desired wages, hours, and working conditions. On the other hand, both men insisted, workers had a right *not* to join a union without being denied employment. Other workers had no right to interfere with this freedom. Any attempt to do so, said Hoar, was "pure despotism" and was destructive of republican liberty and government alike.[37]

The real problem in labor-capital relations, the senators believed, was the failure of the two sides to recognize their interdependence and mutual interests. Instead, as Hoar put it, each "seems to think that it is reason enough for opposing anything which is proposed if the other wants it." Conflicts could be minimized, Platt argued, with mutual recognition and action on the principles of "just dealing between man and man." Certainly, this emphasis on the unity of interest between capital and labor reflected the simpler conditions of their youth.[38]

Ever since the Pullman strike and the Debs case of the 1890s, organized labor had been seeking protection from the injunction and from the application of the Sherman Antitrust Act to unions. During the debate on the Sherman bill, Hoar had expressed concern that labor organizations were being prosecuted under its terms. On December 9, 1901, he introduced a bill to limit the use of injunctions, and to restrict the meaning of the word "conspiracy" to exclude legitimate labor activities. The bill went to the Judiciary Committee, from which Hoar reported it favorably the following February.[39]

Platt's intense opposition to the bill surfaced at once. Hoar refused to take it up for discussion because his Connecticut colleague was ill and absent from the Senate. With Platt so opposed, said Hoar, it "would hardly be fair" to make him come in or to consider the bill in his absence. Hoar hoped Platt would change his mind about the bill, but his colleague continued to oppose such a law. After Hoar's death, Platt recalled the "exceedingly sharp contest" he had had with him on the matter. Hoar, "without reason, seemed to feel that it was a personal controversy, and said some things, which, if not offensive, were extremely exasperating...." In fact, Senator John C. Spooner, also opposed to an anti-injunction law, was so offended that he resigned from the Judiciary Committee altogether, leaving Platt "to bear the brunt of the contest alone."[40]

As in the case of his antiturst bill, Hoar considered his injunction-conspiracy bill a conservative measure, and he defended it as a reinforcement of traditional legal practice. But while Massachusetts labor organizations applauded it, businesses, to Hoar's great annoyance, regarded it as an invitation to anarchy and union "bulldozing" of workers and employers alike.[41]

Hoar could not understand the vehement opposition to his bill. It arose, he suspected, either from misunderstanding the bill's purpose or "perhaps from some very malicious and very silly editorials in the *New York Sun*." He explained carefully to each critic the bill's origin in historical practice. It was modeled on an English law of 1874, drawn by the Lord Chancellor, "a very learned lawyer" and "an exceedingly conservative person." In content, it simply restated the 1844 opinion of Massachusetts Chief Justice Lemuel Shaw, "as conservative a judge as ever sat on a bench and as careful of the rights of capital and of the interests of law and order as any judge that ever lived." Hoar "had not supposed that lawlessness had prevailed in Massachusetts" as a result of Shaw's decision. His bill provided only that acts "lawful and justifiable" when done by one individual should not be criminal when done by several acting together. If workingmen banded together for their interests, as capitalists did for theirs, and did nothing unlawful, it should not be deemed a conspiracy.[42]

Platt could not see it that way. Labor organizations, he was determined, should be as much subject to the Sherman Antitrust Act as were capital combinations. Illegal labor combinations (such as strikes against public carriers) should be "dealt with, with the same justice and the same vigor" as illegal business combinations. "There is no distinction between capital and labor in this matter," Platt declared. Thus, the senator would brook no legislation to limit the law's "vigor" against labor organizations. An anti-injunction law, he wrote, was not "right in principle, or for the interest of the workingmen."[43]

The root of Platt's opposition to such legislation was his overriding determination to preserve social order in the face of widespread unrest and rapid change. Notwithstanding his criticism of capital abuses, he saw a more immediate threat from society's protestors in these years, perhaps because of the violence frequently associated with them. In any case, he once observed that the industrial-combination movement had one consequence especially "to be dreaded and feared." It was "that the workingmen will not respect the interests or the rights of the capitalists."[44] Unlike Hoar, who moved to protect social order with conservative reform, Platt tended, in his later years, to view nearly all reform as a surrender to society's enemies.[45]

A number of characteristics shaped and defined the conservatism of Senators Hoar and Platt; an essential part of which was their instinctive distrust of radicalism and extremism in any form. Both men sought caution, moderation, and "common sense" in all their dealings. Their view of the proper role of the Senate embodied these values. While the Senate stood for the will of the people, Hoar once wrote, it stood for "its deliberate, permanent, settled desire—its sober, second thought." The Senate protected the country from the influence of popular excitement and the passions of the moment. Neither man could abide attempts to pressure the Senate or himself. To succumb to such pressure without trying "to get things right," Platt informed a critic, would violate his duty as a senator. "The Senate is here to do its duty, and not to be swept off its feet by what people may think about it." Hoar was likewise much annoyed when told of certain "demands of the business community." No one had the right to make "demands," he shot back. "It is the Senator's duty to ascertain if he can the interests of the whole country and to act in such a manner as in his judgment will promote those interests."[46]

The desire of these men for moderation colored their responses to the stresses of their time. Extremists in any cause, however righteous, were anathema. Hoar even criticized the radical abolitionists on that point. Planted "on abstract righteousness," they "refused to cooperate with anybody that did not go with them to the extremist length of their belief, and demanded the destruction of the country itself. . . ." That man, warned Hoar, who refused moderate, practical reform because it fell short of his higher ideals was as harmful to the Republic as the worst corruptionist. The rigidly moralistic mugwumps fell into this category, the senator felt, and he fought a running, often bitter, battle with them throughout his career. In fact, he detested them. When someone suggested a memorial lectureship at Harvard in E. L. Godkin's honor, Hoar's answer was biting: "I do not think that should be done until a statue of General Butler has been placed in the State House and some suitable memorial of William M. Tweed has been erected in New York." To Hoar, the definition of a mugwump was one who "has no tolerance of the right of other men to form their own opinions." Their intolerance and self-righteousness made such people poor judges of the character of other men and of the interests of the nation.[47]

During the furor over trusts in the 1890s, Platt expressed his belief in moderation and his perception of a conservative's role.

While he recognized the problems of capital aggregations, "the real truth lies as always between the extremes. The American Commune is as dangerous as capitalistic monopoly." The solutions of sensible men would satisfy neither extreme, "and our only hope is that the good sense of truly conservative men will conserve things." This is what he tried to do.[48]

Platt and Hoar were very "American" conservatives. Both basically optimistic, they believed in progress as an inevitable part of the working out of history. Even in what he regarded as America's most shameful hour—the crushing of Philippine independence—Hoar could still speak of the progress of the human race and of his nation. Errors were being made in his day, certainly, and yet "our generation is better than those who went before it." Future generations would be even better. As the republic was better than the monarchy, so the American Republic "is better than any other Republic. To-day is better than yesterday, and tomorrow will be better than to-day." The human race had made great strides during the past century and, Hoar believed, would "go on more rapidly . . . during the next." Still, his belief in progress was conservative. As he told a Socialist, the great achievements of human history had been accomplished "by a very slow growth indeed. So let us have the patience of God."[49]

Platt was even more convinced of national progress than was Hoar because, unlike his colleague, he saw no shadows on it. He gloried in America's industrial progress and saw her territorial expansion as another stage in her ongoing development. Only now, it would be extended to the world. The United States would foster world progress. America, said Platt in 1902, in defense of her Philippine policies, had "a high call to duty, to a moral duty, to a duty to advance the cause of free government in the world by something more than example." This nation was "a providentially appointed agent" to Christianize the world and convert it to the cause of free government.[50]

On the question of imperialism, Platt's conservatism was lost in his prideful nationalism. He abdicated the preservative role. Hoar remained the true conservative as he tried to hold his country to its traditions and founding principles. On this issue more than any other, the two men were most deeply divided. While Platt looked only to a future of continual progress, Hoar wished to maintain integrity with the past. In the end, each saw a different meaning in the national heritage.

Speaking in 1902, Hoar remarked sadly on the change in American nationalism in recent years. "The orator of to-day puts his emphasis on Glory, on Empire, on Power, on Wealth." Although we lived under the same flag as the fathers, it seemed now to have a different meaning. "We no longer speak of it, except coldly and formally, as the symbol of Liberty; but only as the symbol of power, or of a false, cheap, tinsel glory." To Hoar, that was a perversion of America itself. The present generation, he feared, "so far as the love of liberty is concerned will be known in history as the missing link."[51]

For Hoar, with his deep sense of history, America's true meaning lay in the principles of the past. During the 1898 Senate debate on the Treaty of Paris annexing the Philippine Islands, he confronted Senator Platt on just that question. Platt had spoken at length in defense of America's right and duty to take the islands. Toward the end of his speech, Hoar asked Platt whether he believed that "governments derive their just powers from the consent of the governed?" Platt answered simply and without hesitation: "From the consent of some of the governed." He explained that the states excluded various categories of people from the vote. But for the Massachusetts senator, this was no answer. The words and spirit of the Declaration of Independence were absolutes, especially when they involved the right of nations to self-government. And so he answered Platt: "Does the Senator from Connecticut seriously claim that the great doctrine which is at the foundation of our Revolution and the Declaration of Independence is a falsehood; that it should be qualified by saying governments derive their just powers from the consent of some of the governed, and that the violation of that principle in regard to 10,000,000 people, without any discrimination between ignorance and intelligence, is justified by the reading and writing clause of some of our State constitutions?"[52]

Platt saw no violation of principle. He had unbounded faith in his nation, its future, and its inherent decency. It had a mission to "relieve the oppressed" and extend free government to the world. The American Government and people could "be trusted to do right, and to guarantee to all men who shall come under its beneficent sway and be subject to its jurisdiction the largest measure of liberty consistent with good order and their general well-being."[53]

But to Hoar, the United States, by its own principles, *on record*, had no right to "guarantee" or grant anything if it be done without the consent of the people concerned. This was the heart of the matter. "The Doctrine of 1776 . . . planted our Country on the eternal principles of equality of individuals and of nations in political rights, and declared that no man and no people had the right to judge the fitness of any other for self-government." Freedom was a whole cloth, the same everywhere and in time, whether it applied to slaves, to women denied the suffrage, or to Filipinos fighting for the "independence which is inseparable from the liberty which is the privilege of a free people."[54]

Thus, Hoar fought the annexation of the Philippines and the subsequent war that "crushed their republic" and blocked them on their *own* "road to orderly liberty." He fought American policies that repressed civil liberties in the islands (such as the edict on treason and the law forbidding advocacy of independence) because they violated our own constitutional principles.[55] Again, he came up against Senator Platt, who defended the nation's right to suppress any rebellion against its authority, just as he had asserted its inherent right as a sovereign nation to acquire territory. "Every nation," Platt wrote in 1903, "must, in the course of events, acquire territory, and to my mind, the duty of a nation so acquiring territory is to provide for the people inhabiting it, the best possible government. Any other course would practically put a nation at a standstill. . . ."[56]

In Platt's opinion, the United States was fulfilling its moral duty and national destiny in the Philippines.[57] To Hoar, the nation had betrayed its heritage. Yet both men appealed to part of the spirit of America. Platt proclaimed the nation's confidence in itself. He invoked its sense of destiny and expressed its growing national pride and assertiveness. Hoar, on the other hand, appealed to something more fragile and vulnerable—the spirit of America's free institutions inherited from the past.

The conservatism of George Frisbie Hoar and Orville H. Platt evoked their responses to the Progressive era. Like many Progressives, they viewed issues in moral terms but drew different conclusions as to specific policies. The hallmark of their conservatism was moderation and caution in a time of social stress and demands for economic reform. With Platt, caution often led to resistance to specific reform ideas. Hoar supported moderate, limited reform action. But both men can be termed "centralizing conservatives" for their willingness to use government to achieve their ends. These goals included the promotion of economic growth, the preservation of the social and economic order, and stability. Thus, each accepted some regulation of the economy, although they disagreed about the proper nature and extent of it. Always they had in mind the preservation of the existing political system and the social and economic order (including individual opportunity) that underpinned it. Finally, a deep faith in progress colored their conservatism. And they shared this belief with many Americans, conservative and Progressive alike.

Both men took great pride in the United States, but their nationalism took very different forms. In Platt's case, it led him away from traditional conservatism. Hoar's nationalism, based on the principles of the past, made him an example of the best that conservative thought had to offer in the Progressive era.

Conservatives of the late nineteenth and early twentieth centuries fell into two categories. Decentralizing conservatives, the smaller group, opposed any role for the federal government beyond the traditional laissez-faire functions of preserving order and maintaining the currency on an unsullied gold standard. Centralizing conservatives, such as Hoar and Platt, were ready to expand the role of government for certain purposes. This group included a spectrum of practicing politicians; among them were some of the Senate's most powerful members. As with Platt and Hoar, they differed considerably on the extent of government action they found acceptable.

Platt and Hoar reflected the mainstream of Gilded Age Republicanism. But during the Progressive era, the two men became less representative of the party as a whole. Platt's rigidity against even the moderate reforms of Theodore Roosevelt pushed him into the very conservative wing of the party. Hoar's opposition to imperialism and his continuing concern for black rights separated him from the majority of Republicans. Both men felt out of phase with their time. Hoar expressed his sense of isolation frequently. Platt did so very rarely, but it was still there. Just a few months before his death, while embroiled in struggles over tariff revision, railroad rate regulation, and the pure-food bill, Platt took a philosophical look at his position. "There are tendencies now which I do not like very well," he wrote, "and yet I question whether or not I am too much of an old fogy to keep up with the procession, or whether the procession is really moving too fast."[58]

NOTES

1. For a discussion of mugwumps as conservatives rather than as "liberal reformers," see Edwina C. Smith, "Conservatism in the Gilded Age: The Senatorial Career of Orville H. Platt" (Ph.D. diss., University of North Carolina, 1976), pp. 242-43, 342.

2. Gerald W. McFarland, *Mugwumps, Morals and Politics, 1884-1920* (Amherst, Mass.: University of Massachusetts Press, 1975), pp. 107-21, 143-44, 146.

3. Hoar entered in 1877; Platt, in 1879.

4. Louis A. Coolidge, *An Old Fashioned Senator: Orville H. Platt of Connecticut* (New York and London: G. P. Putnam's Sons, 1910), pp. 5-10.

5. George Frisbie Hoar, *Autobiography of Seventy Years* (New York: Charles Scribner's Sons, 1903), 1:16-17, 24-25, 30-31, 132.

6. *Boston Herald*, Jan. 7, 1903, and Howard W. Allen and Jerome Clubb, "Progressive Reform and the Political System," *Pacific Northwest Quarterly* 65 (July 1974): 135-36.

7. For federal aid to education, see *Congressional Record*, 48th Cong., 1st sess., pp. 2071, 2710, 2712-13, 2720, 2724; ibid., 49th Cong., 1st sess., pp. 1778, 2105; *Connecticut Courant*, Mar. 13, 1890; Daniel W. Crofts, "The Black Response to the Blair Education Bill," *Journal of Southern History* 37 (February 1971): 53. For the Federal Elections Bill, see O. H. Platt to A. H. Kellam, Aug. 18, 1890, in Coolidge, *Platt*, pp. 232-34; George F. Hoar, "Party Government in the United States: The Importance of Government by the Republican Party," *International Quarterly* 2 (October 1900): 426-27; George Frisbie Hoar, "The Fate of the Election Bill," *The Forum* 11 (April 1891): 127-36; and *Connecticut Courant*, Aug. 21, 1890.

8. George F. Hoar to George T. Downing, Jan. 27, 1902, George Frisbie Hoar Papers, Massachusetts Historical Society, Boston; Richard E. Welch, Jr., *Response to Imperialism: The United States and the Philippine-American War, 1899-1902* (Chapel Hill: University of North Carolina Press, 1979), p. 106; and Hoar to Rev. Reverdy C. Ransom, Mar. 11, 1903, Hoar Papers.

9. O. H. Platt to Samuel A. Green, Jan. 29, 1898, Samuel A. Green Papers, Massachusetts Historical Society: *Meriden Morning Record*, Oct. 27, 1892; H. Huntington to O. H. Platt, Sept. 20, 1903, Platt to John H. Flagg, Mar. 30, 1905, Platt to Robert N. Jackson, Jan. 31, 1903, O. H. Platt Papers, Connecticut State Library, Hartford; *Boston Herald*, Jan. 7, 1903; and Hoar to Charles S. Vedder, Feb. 4, 1903, Hoar Papers.

10. *Boston Herald*, Dec. 23, 1902; and Hoar to William H. Hart, Jan. 24, 1903, Hoar Papers.

11. Richard E. Welch, Jr., *George Frisbie Hoar and the Half-Breed Republicans* (Cambridge: Harvard University Press, 1971), pp. 6-7, 176, 294-95, 315-17, and McFarland, *Mugwumps, Morals and Politics*, p. 147.

12. *Congressional Record*, 53rd Cong., 2d sess., p. 6704, and *Report of the Senate Select Committee on Interstate Commerce*, S. Rept. 46, pt. 2 (s.n. 2357), 49th Cong., 1st sess., p. 931.

13. Welch, *Hoar*, p. 166; *Congressional Record*, 57th Cong., 2d sess., pp. 520-21, 523; Hoar to Henry A. Marsh, Apr. 3, 1903, Hoar Papers; and memorandum of conversation with Roosevelt, Nov. 13, 1903, in Hoar Papers.

14. *Congressional Record*, 49th Cong., 2d sess., p. 364. For Hoar, see Welch, *Hoar*, p. 31.

15. For a detailed comparison of Aldrich and Platt as conservatives, see Edwina C. Smith, "Two Conservative Approaches to Politics in the 1890s: Nelson W. Aldrich and Orville H. Platt" (M.A. thesis, University of North Carolina, 1970).

16. Coolidge, *Platt*, pp. 12, 432; *Congressional Record*, 57th Cong., 2d sess., p. 519; and ibid., 53rd Cong., 2d sess., p. 5028.

17. Ibid., 57th Cong., 2d sess., pp. 519, 521-22.

18. Theodore Roosevelt to Platt, Sept. 30, 1901, Mar. 16, 1903, Sept. 11, 1903, June 29, 1904, Aug. 1, 1904, Aug. 29, 1904, Sept. 5, 1904, Theodore Roosevelt Papers, Manuscript Division, Library of Congress; Platt to Roosevelt, Nov. 13, 1901, May 23, 1904, Sept. 2, 1904, Sept. 23, 1904, Roosevelt Papers; and Platt to Nelson W. Aldrich, Aug. 17, 1903, Nelson W. Aldrich Papers, Manuscript Division, Library of Congress.

19. *Boston Evening Transcript*, Dec. 4, 1901. Hoar objected to the section on Chinese exclusion because it excluded "persons however fit because of their race or because they are laborers." He wrote privately: "Let the admission or exclusion be determined by individual worth not by occupation." Hoar to Francis P. Silver, Dec. 18, 1901, Hoar to N. R. Johnston, Jan. 10, 1902, Hoar Papers. Hoar had objected to anti-Chinese legislation for decades. See *Congressional Record*, 48th Cong., 1st sess., p. 5938, and Hoar to Horace Gray, May 16, 1893, Horace Gray Papers, Manuscript Division, Library of Congress.

20. *Boston Evening Transcript*, Dec. 4, 1901. On Mabini, see Hoar to Fiske Warren, Dec. 22, 1902, Hoar to Moorfield Storey, Feb. 5, 1903, Hoar Papers; *Boston Herald*, Dec. 23, 1902, Jan. 15, 1903. On the Philippine investigation, see Hoar to Secretary of War Elihu Root, Jan. 14, 1901, Isaac Bridgman, Jan. 16, 1902, Hoar to Bridgman, Jan. 18, 1902, Hoar to Phoebe W. Couzins, Jan. 18, 1902, Hoar to Nellie Louise Hill, Apr. 8, 1902, Hoar to Mrs. C. R. Lowell, Dec. 29, 1902, Hoar Papers. For Panama, see "Senator Hoar and the President," *The Nation* 77 (December 24, 1903): 496, and "Senator Hoar's Speech," *The Outlook* 75 (December 26, 1903): 982-84.

21. Hoar to Fiske Warren, Dec. 22, 1902, Hoar to Charles S. Vedder, Feb. 4, 1903, Hoar Papers.

22. Reminiscence recorded by Kathleen Lawler (Platt's personal secretary), Nov. 2, 1904, Platt Papers, and Platt to William E. Chandler, Sept. 23, 1904, Platt Papers.

23. Some historians of the period argue that progressivism was really a counterrevolution against radical change. If this view is accepted, Hoar and Platt should perhaps be regarded as counterrevolutionaries to a more extreme degree. For a discussion of this view of progressivism, see Allen and Clubb, "Progressive Reform and the Political System."

24. *Report of the Senate Select Committee on Interstate Commerce*, p. 643; Platt to Wharton Barker, Nov. 15, 1892, Wharton Barker Papers, Manuscript Division, Library of Congress; and Platt to John H. Flagg, Nov. 14, 1904, Mar. 30, 1905, Platt Papers.

25. Welch, *Hoar*, p. 309. A year later, however, Hoar referred to the "sense of relief" occasioned when the dangers resulting from the strike were averted "by the wisdom of President Roosevelt." Hoar to C. W. Hobbs, Feb. 22, 1904, Hoar Papers. Platt to William J. Clark, Nov. 30, 1903, to E. H. Van Ingen, Dec. 14, 1903, to James R. Winchell, Dec. 16, 1903, to John H. Flagg, Dec. 30, 1903, Feb. 5, 1904, to Charles S. Mellen, Jan. 25, 1904, and Mellen to Platt, Jan. 25, 1904, Platt Papers.

26. *Boston Evening Transcript*, Dec. 18, 1902. For his role in preparing the Sherman Antitrust Act, see Hoar to Thomas M. Cooley, Jan. 10, 1889, Thomas M. Cooley Papers, Michigan Historical Collections, University of Michigan (copy in possession of author); Hoar to Henry Wade Rogers, Nov. 12, 1901, Henry Wade Rogers Papers, Michigan Historical Collections (copy in possession of author); "Address Delivered Before the New England Society of Pennsylvania," Dec. 22, 1902, p. 26, manuscript in Hoar Papers; and Hoar to Joseph Nimmo, Jan. 31, 1903, Hoar Papers.

27. Hoar to G. Stanley Hall, Dec. 29, 1902, Hoar to F. W. Pitcher, Jan. 10, 1903, Hoar Papers.

28. *Congressional Record*, 57th Cong., 2d sess., pp. 518-20, 523; Hoar to Philander Knox, Jan. 3, 1903, Hoar Papers; and "Address Delivered Before New England Society of Pennsylvania," pp. 31-32, Hoar Papers.

29. *Boston Evening Transcript*, Dec. 18, 19, 1902; *Boston Herald*, Jan. 7, 1903; and Welch, *Hoar*, p. 307.

30. *Congressional Record*, 53rd Cong., 2d sess., p. 6704; "The Connecticut Republican Platform, with Senator O. H. Platt's Statement of Republican Policy and Doctrine," *American Monthly Review of Reviews* 26 (October 1902); 452-53; and *Congressional Record*, 57th Cong., 2d sess., p. 2299.

31. Ibid., pp. 520-21.

32. Ibid., 53rd Cong., 2d sess., pp. 6701-06. Hoar stated in his trust-bill speech: "I have no sympathy with any attack on wealth honorably

acquired and lawfully used." *Congressional Record*, 57th Cong., 2d sess., p. 521.

33. Platt to John H. Flagg, Mar. 10, 1905, Platt Papers.

34. Hoar to William F. Draper, Jan. 10, 1903, Hoar Papers.

35. *Congressional Record*, 51st Cong., 1st sess., pp. 2607-08; ibid., 56th Cong., 2d sess., p. 2729; ibid., 57th Cong., 2d sess., p. 2299; Platt to Theodore Roosevelt, Nov. 13, 1901, Roosevelt Papers; and *Congressional Record*, 57th Cong., 2d sess., p. 523.

36. Platt to Wharton Barker, Nov. 15, 1902, Barker Papers; Platt to C. S. Mellen, Dec. 12, 1904, Platt to Lucius Tuttle, Jan. 18, 1905, Samuel Dodd to Platt, Jan. 31, 1905, Platt to Samuel Dodd, Feb. 2, 1905, Platt to S. C. Dunham, Feb. 2, 1905, Platt Papers; and *Congressional Record*, 53rd Cong., 2d sess., pp. 4066-67.

37. Speech by Platt to Hartford Workingmen's Club, 1904, in Coolidge, *Platt*, pp. 431-33, and Hoar's "Address Delivered Before the New England Society of Pennsylvania," pp. 43-44, Hoar Papers.

38. Hoar to C. W. Hobbs, Feb. 22, 1904, Hoar Papers, and Coolidge, *Platt*, p. 432.

39. Alpheus T. Mason, *Organized Labor and the Law, with Especial Reference to the Sherman and Clayton Acts* (Durham: Duke University Press, 1925), pp. 123-26; *Congressional Record*, 57th Cong., 1st sess., p. 212; and Hoar to J. F. Callahan, Feb. 5, 1902, Hoar Papers.

40. *Congressional Record*, 57th Cong., 1st sess., p. 1451, and Platt to Albert J. Beveridge, Nov. 21, 1904, Platt Papers.

41. Examples of labor support are: H. E. Daniels et al. to Hoar, Jan. 20, 1902, W. S. Shaw to Hoar, Mar. 10, 1902, and Henry E. Strout et al. to Hoar (1902), Hoar Papers. For business opposition, see M. T. Richardson to Hoar, Feb. 6, 1902, Edwin T. Marble to Hoar, Mar. 1, 1902, E. E. Keller to Hoar, Mar. 3, 1902, Holyoke Machine Co. to Hoar, Mar. 5, 1902, L. J. Larzelere to Hoar, Mar. 6, 1902, Rufus B. Fowler to Hoar, Apr. 2, 1902, Hoar Papers.

42. Hoar to Holyoke Machine Co., Mar. 7, 1902, to T. J. Hurley, Feb. 17, 1904, to Edwin T. Marble, Mar. 5, 1902, to M. T. Richardson, Feb. 7, 1902, to Rufus B. Fowler, Apr. 7, 1902, Hoar Papers.

43. *Congressional Record*, 53rd Cong., special sess. of the Senate, pp. 119-20, and Platt to George W. Saunders, Dec. 16, 1903, Platt Papers.

44. *Congressional Record*, 53rd Cong., 2d sess., p. 5028.

45. The two senators also parted company over the federal eight-hour-day bill. Hoar had favored shorter hours legislation for decades and had supported the bill. See Hoar, *Autobiography*, 1:163-64; Hoar to George E. Wadleigh, Jan. 11, 1901, to C. H. Bell, Dec. 30, 1902, to George A. Keene, Dec. 31, 1902, Hoar Papers. Platt successfully fought the bill during 1902 and 1904 on the grounds that it would force businesses to give up their government contracts, thus curtailing employment for workers. See Platt

to C. E. Newton, Feb. 5, 1904, to Henry G. Thresher, Mar. 22, 1904, to R. B. Foley, Mar. 11, 1904, Platt Papers.

46. George F. Hoar, "Has the Senate Degenerated?" *The Forum* 23 (April 1897): 142; newspaper clipping (1902), Hoar Papers; Platt to Charles Hopkins Clark, Feb. 13, 1905, in Coolidge, *Platt*, p. 464; and Hoar to Edward Atkinson, Feb. 4, 1902, Hoar Papers.

47. Hoar, "Party Government in the United States," pp. 424, 430, 433-34; Hoar to James C. Carter, Feb. 5, 1903, to Charles A. Moody, Apr. 15, 1904, to Edward Atkinson, Jan. 25, 1901, Hoar Papers; and Hoar, "Has the Senate Degenerated?" p. 144.

48. Platt to Wharton Barker, June 17, 1891, Barker Papers.

49. "Address Delivered at Chicalawbut Club," Boston, 1902, p. 7, manuscript in Hoar Papers, and Hoar to Loring Puffer, Jan. 2, 1902, Hoar to H. Gaylord Wilshire, Jan. 9, 1903, Hoar Papers.

50. *Congressional Record*, 57th Cong., 1st sess., p. 1589.

51. "Address to Chicalawbut Club," p. 8, Hoar Papers, and Hoar to Isaac Bridgman, Jan. 18, 1902, Hoar Papers.

52. *Congressional Record*, 55th Cong., 3d sess., p. 297.

53. Ibid.

54. Ibid., p. 503; Hoar to Charles Francis Adams, Dec. 27, 1901, Hoar Papers; "Address to Chicalawbut Club," p. 7, Hoar Papers; and Hoar to Henry B. Blackwell, Dec. 23, 1901, Hoar to General Thomas M. Anderson, Jan. 22, 1902, Hoar Papers.

55. Hoar to Nathan Henry Warren, Feb. 24, 1902, Hoar to C. E. D. Phelps, Feb. 14, 1902, Hoar Papers, and *Congressional Record*, 57th Cong., 1st sess., pp. 1590-91.

56. Ibid., p. 1588, and Platt to W. Wallace Lee, Mar. 28, 1903, Platt Papers.

57. See "The Connecticut Republican Platform, with Senator O. H. Platt's Statement of Republican Policy and Doctrine," p. 452, and "Republican Achievement," speech of Senator O. H. Platt at the Connecticut Republican State Convention, Sept. 13, 1904, copy in Connecticut State Library, Hartford.

58. Platt to Charles F. Brooker, Jan. 16, 1905, Platt Papers.

7

REFORM AND RADICALISM: JOHN REED AND THE LIMITS OF REFORM

Robert A. Rosenstone

In American history, the name John Reed is synonymous with radicalism, both cultural and political. Between 1910 and 1917, the first great era of Bohemianism in this country, he was one of the heroes of Greenwich Village, a man equally renowned as satiric poet and tough-minded short-story writer; as dashing reporter, contributing editor of *The Masses*, and cofounder of the Provinceton Players; as lover of attractive women like Mabel Dodge, and friend of the notorious such as Bill Haywood, Emma Goldman, Margaret Sanger, and Pancho Villa. When the repression attendant upon United States participation in World War I destroyed Bohemia and devastated the ranks of American political radicals, Reed moved onto a global stage, became a chronicler of the Russian revolution, an associate of Trotsky and Lenin, and a member of the Executive Committee of the Communist International. He died of typhus in Moscow in 1920, was buried before the Kremlin wall, and ever since, has been more honored in the Soviet Union than in his homeland.[1]

The man who engaged in so much notorious activity was a product of a solid middle-class family, one in which radicalism was not so much despised as simply unacknowledged or unknown. Like most Bohemians of his generation, Reed's heritage and upbringing were genteel; his family politics, those of reform; and his personal ambitions, enormous. His father was a Progressive, and one of young Reed's first heroes was Theodore Roosevelt. From an early age, his aim was to be successful and famous. That such a wellencultured young man should follow a path toward martyrdom in Russia, not only says much about him, but also provides an interesting perspective on the first two decades of the twentieth century, and on the theme of reform so central to American life in that era. Reed was part of a broad, inchoate movement in which some children of the liberal middle classes were—in the name of freedom and self-expression—testing and finding inadequate the behavior patterns and beliefs of their parents. To study his development is to gain insight into this movement—sometimes called a "generational revolt"—to see how it both derives from a middle-class heritage and highlights the limits of the mentality of reform.[2]

Caution is in order when one sets about to use biography to suggest lessons of a broad historical nature. Reed was a rare individual, an exceptionally talented writer, and the only one of his middle-class peers to die for a cause. Yet from the perspective adopted here, neither personal accomplishments nor final commitments are most important. Rather, the concern is with the representative of the prewar radical, artistic subculture that, for want of a better term, we label "Bohemia." In this realm—a hodgepodge of university-spawned intellectuals, avant-garde poets and visual artists, European-born and native radicals, feminists, advocates of birth control and free love, Marxists, anarchists, and cubists—Reed was alternately admired, envied, and resented. But in the midteens, nobody doubted that he was already, as Walter Lippmann proclaimed, "legendary."[3] As such a legend, or culture hero, he experienced in full the ideals, tensions, contradictions, and liberations of the subculture that nurtured and honored him.

To be precise about the critique of reform that emerges from John Reed's life, or the generational shift in attitude that it represents, one must tidy up history even more than usual. The notion of a "reform mentality" is elusive enough, and failure would seem to hover over any attempt to make coherent those sprawling, unsystematic, and self-contradictory beliefs that characterize Bohemia in pre-World War I days. Yet behind the artistic, political, and intellectual clashes, the competing claims of many isms, the faddish cries for the new in art, sex, politics, lifestyle, dress, dance, and modes of self-reflection, one can discern commonalities, sense certain tentative gropings away from some cultural patterns and toward others. Here is a dividing line—not sharp or precise, but visible nonetheless—between parents and children, past and future, which suggests that Reed's contemporaries were forerunners of what later be called a counterculture; that is, a subculture whose values call into question not only reform politics but the entire world view we term "bourgeois."

Central to such a world view are the following three beliefs, rooted so deeply in the culture that reformers and Progressives could accept them as virtually self-evident truths: that competitive economic individualism is the engine of personal and social progress; that the ideas and morals of WASP Americans are superior to those of the working class, immigrants, and all foreign cultures; that the practical and instrumental constitute the best possible approach to social and political life. It was just such notions that the younger generation was calling into question. Among Reed's peers, one observes a disdain for economic competition and a desire for some form of extended family or community; a belief that the lower classes at home and abroad are morally equal, and in some ways superior, to those who lord it over them economically, politically, and culturally; and a tendency to make aesthetic judgments—broadly construed—take precedence over practical ones. Naturally, such attitudes helped to fuel the revolutionary politics that most visibly set Reed off from the tradition of reform.

To trace this shift of attitudes, equal attention must be paid to Reed's writings and behavior, for he was a man whose mode of expression included action as well as words. Bumptious, aggressive, and self-centered, he nonetheless shared with many contemporaries both a liberation from parental views and the agony that the received wisdom of his elders could neither explain nor justify the historical changes he witnessed and experienced. This process helped to create the texture of all Reed's days, but for purposes of this argument, it is only necessary to focus on certain aspects and incidents of his career. The strategy is as follows: first, to gain an overview of his life; then, to see how it serves to highlight the limitations of reform.

John Reed's life began quite literally at the top. Born in 1877, his early years were spent at Cedar Hill, a five-acre estate overlooking Portland, Oregon. A mansion had been built there by his maternal grandfather, Henry Green, one of the city's founders and a pioneer capitalist of extravagant tastes whose descendants had turned ultra-respectable in one generation. With such a background, Reed was indulged as a youth, and he attended a private academy in Portland before going off to Morristown Prep School and then to Harvard. For his mother, herself the product of an eastern finishing school, the aim of such an education was to make her son acceptable in the "best circles" anywhere in the United States. For young Jack, going east promised freedom from the straight-laced provincialism of his hometown and provided an arena in which to test himself. At the age of sixteen, he was determined to be a writer, and he well understood that in the world of letters, fame and fortune came only to those who were on the East Coast.

A lack of political concerns in Reed's classical education were offset by his father's firsthand involvements. Businessman Charles Jerome Reed, a strong believer in honesty in both public and private life, was not a man to avoid a call to conscience. In 1905, he entered the world of reform politics by accepting an appointment as U.S. marshall from Francis J. Heney, a special prosecutor selected by Theodore Roosevelt to investigate fraud in Northwest timber lands. For three years, Heney and Reed did their job so well that some of the leading political and social figures in Oregon were either prosecuted, convicted, or implicated in the illegal dealings. All this activity made C. J. something of a pariah among his associates, and it sharply curtailed his livelihood. But it also wedded him more firmly to reform. In 1910, he ran unsuccessfully for Congress as a Progressive, and two years later, he was active in the abortive movement to help Roosevelt wrest the Republican nomination away from President Taft.

The politics that were central to the last years of C. J.'s life—he died suddenly of a stroke in 1912—touched his son deeply but did little in the short run to affect his behavior. They helped to make Reed see his father as a hero; but at college between 1906 and 1910, he exhibited little concern with local, state, or national affairs beyond those that involved C. J. During that period, Harvard was struck by what Reed would later call an "influx of discontent, of revolutionary ideas, of criticism and revolt."[4] Part of the normally complacent student body, responding to the reformers and radicals who had been stirring America for a decade, became passionate about social issues and created numerous political organizations that, first, agitated for change on campus and, then, attempted to influence local and state politics. Their concerns touched Reed but little. Occasionally, he attended meetings of these groups, but in general, he found them less important than his role in Harvard's literary world—managing the Drama Club, helping to edit the *Lampoon* and the *Monthly*—and infinitely less compelling than his position as football cheerleader.

Graduation left Reed free to gravitate to Manhattan—by 1910, the cultural as well as financial capital of the nation. At first, his lot was that of the fledgling writer; money came from journalistic pieces and editorial duties on popular magazines. But the most important part of life was the attempt to find a personal voice in poetry, fiction, and drama. A quick success in the commercial world, Reed was annoyed and dismayed to find that some of his most serious efforts were unacceptable there. These were welcomed by editor Max Eastman into the pages of *The Masses*, a small-circulation, lively, experimental monthly, and soon he was drawn into the realm of artistic, political, and economic radicalism to which and for which it spoke.

In truth, he had been living on the edge of that world for some time. Early in 1911, Reed and several friends had moved into an apartment on Washington Square, in Greenwich Village, the center of a new kind of Bohemia formerly unknown in America, one simultaneously serious and fun-loving, where the worlds of avant-garde art and political radicalism intersected. At that time, the Village was "sending out a call" to sensitive youngsters all over the nation, and they were flocking there to find a community where deviant behavior—such as writing poetry, painting, espousing anarchism, or living together without benefit of clergy—was cherished rather than condemned. Suspicious of the many hangers-on for whom the area was merely a playground, a place to loaf and cadge drinks, Reed was nonetheless at home there. In 1913, he won a large measure of local fame for the privately printed, lengthy narrative poem, *The Day in Bohemia*, which helped to capture and define the lifestyle of that generation.[5]

For the next four years, Reed was a central figure in Bohemia without ever losing his strong position in the high-paying realm of commercial magazines. So enormous were his drive and energy that the range of his activities can only be suggested: he was an editor of and frequent contributor to *The Masses*; a highly paid correspondent for the mass-circulation *Metropolitan Magazine*; an author of poems, plays, humorous sketches, book reviews, and short stories both commercial and serious; a crucial force in the creation of the

Provincetown Players on Cape Cod and in that group's removal to New York City; a member of the Liberal Club and a frequenter of Village hangouts such as Polly's, the Brevoort, the Crazy Cat, and the Working Girls' Home; an early resident of the rural colony in Croton; a supporter of feminism and birth control; and a lover of more than a few young women anxious to shed the restrictive bonds of Victorian morality. His best-known liaison was with the wealthy Mabel Dodge, seven years his senior, a woman whose salon was one of the Village's central meeting places.

During those years, artistic issues merged into social and economic ones, and Reed was slowly pulled toward radical politics. He could read about the doctrines of Marxism, socialism, anarchism, and syndicalism in *The Masses*, and hear them debated often enough among friends; but on the whole, words affected him less than the glaring contrast between rich and poor, the sharp evidence of exploitation encountered daily on Manhattan streets. His first political involvement began in April 1913. In response to the impassioned words of "Big Bill" Haywood, the slouchy, battered, theatrical chief of the Industrial Workers of the World (IWW), Reed nipped over to Paterson, New Jersey, to see what he could do to help 25,000 strikers who had shut down the silk mills there. A brash assertion of individual rights to a quick-tempered cop landed Reed in jail, and he emerged four days later with blood in his eye and vitriol on his pen. His commitment to the "Wobblies" was demonstrated in more than the written word. Reed's prodigious efforts were instrumental in bringing to life the Paterson Pageant—simultaneously a propaganda vehicle and money-raising venture for the IWW—on June 7 in Madison Square Garden.

Paterson made Reed notorious; his next radical involvement made him famous. Late in 1913, he accepted assignments from *Metropolitan* and the *New York World* to cover the little-understood events of the revolution then unfolding in Mexico. Unlike many reporters who concocted their stories from rumors circulating in El Paso, Texas, Jack journeyed far south of the border, became friends with Pancho Villa in Chihuahua, rode with a detachment of horseback troops, and joined Villa's footsoldiers when they stormed toward the important victory at Torréon in March 1914. So vivid were his articles from the front that the usually critical Walter Lippmann, in the pages of the *New Republic*, would claim that it was Reed who made America take Villa seriously. In a personal note, he was even more complimentary: "Your . . . articles are undoubtedly the finest reporting that's ever been done. . . . I say that with Jack Reed reporting begins."[6]

Much of the strength of Reed's work derived from his identification with the revolutionaries, whose bravery and beliefs also helped to solidify his commitment to radical politics. This identification clearly showed later in 1914, when, as a now-renowned correspondent on the western front, Jack could not fill his reports with any of the verve and passion that editors expected. The war seemed not only meaningless but also detrimental to artistic and social progress —indeed, to civilization itself. It taught Reed that he could only be creative when his deepest sympathies were engaged. To see the war, as he now did, as a logical outgrowth of capitalism was to endanger his livelihood. As the United States drifted toward involvement, he was active in the antiwar movement, remaining in opposition even after America's entry in April 1917. By that summer, virtually all commercial outlets were closed to him, and gloom over the course of the world and his professional trials darkened Reed's days.

The Russian revolution saved him from despair. A combination of savvy intuition and financial support from friends landed him in Petrograd in September 1917. Even before the ten days that he would capture in prose, Reed was a Bolshevik partisan, convinced that only they were serious about ending Russia's involvement in the war. The fulfillment of that promise, and the subsequent feverish plans for social reconstruction, wedded him to the revolution. He served briefly as a propagandist in the Soviet Foreign Ministry, then he returned to the United States, where his papers were seized by the government and he was twice forced to stand trial with other *Masses* editors for articles that supposedly interfered with the war effort. Influence from his more famous days helped win the release of his papers, and Reed swiftly wrote *Ten Days That Shook the World*, then hurled himself into the task of bringing revolution to America. His path led from the left wing of the Socialist party to the founding convention of the Communist Labor party (CLP) and then back to Russia in 1919 to plead for Comintern recognition of the CLP. Shortly after the Second Congress of the Communist International, he contracted typhus and died; like millions of Russians, he was a victim of insufficient medical supplies caused by the Allied blockade of the new Russian regime.

To see the limits of reform through Reed's life, one must not fail to notice, first, just how much strength and support he drew from his middle-class background. Both sheltered and indulged as a child, he was encouraged in literary aims by parents who saw no conflict between cultural pursuits and the possibility of making a decent living. From C. J.'s example, he learned about the necessity of standing firm for one's beliefs, and about the cost of rectitude in public affairs. An education at elite schools reinforced those tendencies. Harvard's course-elective system provided evidence that following one's own pathway was the essence of freedom, and the content of its courses led him inevitably to the conclusion that the artifacts of high culture were the noblest products of a civilization.

Such a background encouraged Reed's natural tendency to deal with the world essentially as a poet, as a person ready to seize upon certain aspects of reality and intensify them with the power of art. That it was, by usual standards, hardly a practical way of handling life never bothered him, for he lived in a subculture of like-minded people. Indeed, nothing sets Reed's generation so clearly apart from that of its parents than that these indulged children of the middle class refused to accept the notion that practical considerations always took precedence over aesthetic, playful, dramatic, heroic, experimental, or experiential ones. This is not to say that they were incapable of holding jobs, completing tasks, raising families, or honoring commitments. Rather, it suggests a subtler but still significant point: much less than their parents' generation were Reed's contemporaries bound by the delayed gratification and repression of instincts that lie at the heart of bourgeois culture.

The difference between generations was less one of absolutes than of degrees. Nowhere is this distinction more evident than in the area of competition. As a good child of the middle class, Reed was full of the combativeness and self-assertion necessary in a competitive order. But, as was common among Bohemians, his ambition was not channeled into economic enterprise. Money meant little to him and he was never interested in acquiring material possessions. When affluent, he shared his income with friends and family; when money was in short supply, he easily did without the things it would buy. Such behavior showed that his aim was elsewhere. Reed hungered for success, but as a poet, dramatist, or novelist, in realms where monetary evaluation was largely beside the point.

His pronounced thirst for fame made him an unlikely candidate for communal activities, where the downplaying of self is a prerequisite for group success. Yet, if he was commonly criticized for being self-centered, Reed was not immune to the communitarian impulse that ran through the subculture. During his Harvard days, he enthusiastically endorsed a proposal for a group of creative friends to homestead in the West after graduation and live and work communally. If reality stepped in to squelch such a vision, he soon found himself with many of those same friends in the Village, where the sharing of apartments, income, and personal problems meant that life had more the texture of an extended rather than a nuclear family. This was true of Bohemia as a whole. In restaurants, bars, bookstores, and hangouts like the Liberal Club, Villagers felt —for all their internal quarrels—like a group apart, a family or tribe banded together to defy the curiosity, criticism, scorn, and fascination of middle-class journalists, tourists, moralists, and slummers.

Reed was a force in two Bohemian institutions specifically collective in origin: *The Masses* and the Provincetown Players. An ambivalence over communal activities was most clearly revealed on the magazine; at monthly meetings, he was contentious enough to earn the title "spoiled child" of the editorial board.[7] A recurrent problem centered around the need to accept collective decisions on works of art, which became impossible for him when the work was his own. Reed once submitted a poem under an assumed name, and when it was read aloud and then rejected, he revealed his identity as author and insisted that it be included in the next issue. To calm his anger, the other editors had to agree. By the time the Players were formed, he was less self-assertive. Though the most famous of the founding members, Reed was content to help in such small tasks as building sets, painting scenery, and acting in minor roles, along with the major jobs of writing and directing one-act plays. But it was then the summer of 1916, and the mounting pressure of the world war was already moving Reed toward thoughts of political and social change.

The world of radicalism and revolution most clearly reveals Reed's scorn for economic competition and his impulse toward the collective. Initially unable to deny his own egocentric desires, he could at least want for others what eluded him. Central to all the political movements he loved—the Wobblies, Villistas, and Bolsheviks—was a communtarian vision. Certainly, he was impressed by strong or fiery leaders—by Bill Haywood and Carlo Tresca, by Villa, Lenin, and Trotsky—but his heart went out to the common folk who endured the trials, duties, pain, and joy of social upheaval. His words sang and rose toward poetry in describing the selfless-ness of the Paterson strikers in jail and on the picket line; the camaraderie of Mexican revolutionaries who, accompanied by wives and mistresses, shared water, beans, and tortillas on the battlefields; the masses of workers, peasants, and soldiers who comprised the real "hero of the Russian revolution" and collec-tively proved themselves capable of "inventing a whole new form of civilization."[8] The experience underlying such vision was not without its effect. When Reed was organizing the CLP in 1919, one labor leader noted that he did not, like some other middle-class radicals, "go down to the working class." Rather, he seemed "with it and of it."[9] This comment, and the final and fatal trip to Russia at a time when he was sick and weary, indicated that by the end, Reed was able to put commitments to others ahead of those to himself.

A lifetime might be necessary to tame ambition, but shedding middle-class morality could occur almost overnight. At Harvard, Reed drank and smoked, but, like his classmates, his relations with females were idealized rather than carnal. Less than a year after graduation, however, he was casually spending nights with Village women who seemed unconcerned about protecting their "reputa-tions." Indeed, in Bohemia, morality ran in the opposite direction: young ladies worried about remaining virgins, and couples old-fashioned enough to get married hid that social misdeed and pre-tended to be only living together. In an earlier era, sexual adven-tures might be expected of a young man, but discretion would have been deemed in order. This was not the way of Reed's generation. When sharing Mabel Dodge's villa in Italy or her elegant apartment in New York, he never attempted to conceal the fact. Nor was he secretive when, after his 1915 visit home, Louise Bryant, the wife of a socially prominent dentist, suddenly left Portland and moved into Reed's apartment in the Village. This proved too much for his mother, who refused all invitations to visit the couple and only reconciled with Louise after they were married in 1917.[10]

Not just the behavior of Bohemians offended their elders. Their perpetual concern with sex and their vocal and written stridency were equally dismaying. Unlike some Villagers, Reed was no theorist of free love, but sexual matters could not help but enter his consciousness and his writing. Since childhood, he, like many middle-class youths, had been fascinated by the seamy underside of urban life. The step from the vice-ridden Portland waterfront to Satan's Circus in Manhattan was not a long one, and Reed filled some of his best short stories with sympathetic portraits of crooks, con men, and prostitutes. A supposedly "immoral" tale, in fact, propelled him into the realm of radicalism. He wrote a simple story about a hooker who basically enjoyed her work and was never punished for her transgressions. The story was rejected on moral grounds by popular magazines that had accepted other stories he considered more trivial, and this became Reed's first contribution to *The Masses*.[11]

Magazines that judged Reed's story immoral were expressing a middle-class tradition in which the control of impulses—what Freud calls sublimation—was identified as the basis of civilization itself. In a hierarchy of nations, such control was seen as the measure of Anglo-Saxon superiority; for America to continue growing progressively stronger, a similar morality was deemed necessary for the entire social order. To reformers, secure in their own elevated standards, this morality did not require overt coercion, but the enlightened ways of education, legislation, and propaganda. The target was not just sexual behavior, but all the drinking, singing, gambling, and other frivolous amusements generally identified with the lower classes.

Reed found such attitudes ridiculous. Experiences in immigrant ghettos and in lower-class districts of Manhattan, Paterson, and Lawrence; among Mexican, Italian, and Serbian peasants; and at the homes of French and Russian intellectuals reinforced his own beliefs that sensual pleasure—broadly construed—was part of a wholesome life. To him, the level of a civilization was not marked by its industrial progress, but by its quota of human happiness. This attitude led him to denounce efforts such as the one to protect New York working girls by investigating the evil influence of dancehalls with their supposedly salacious modern steps. Reed believed that these young ladies had their own "sense of beauty," one that reformers should respect. Such an assertion of cultural relativism was only a way station to a more extreme position. Like other Bohemians, Reed sometimes flirted with a kind of primitivism, one that turned tradition upside down. It was easy to idealize what appeared to be the easier sensual behavior of workers, immigrants, and foreigners and then to judge harshly the lives of middle-class elders as repressed, constricted, joyless, and unhealthy.

The quest for happiness was not simply a personal demand; it had a public dimension as well. Reed expected from the social arena the same color and excitement that he sought in private life, and in the decade of his maturity, radical politics was brimming with such possibilities. His reputation may be that of radical writer and activist, but it would be a serious mistake to see him as basically a political animal. The regular activities of that normally practical process—elections, campaigns, coalitions, compromises—never held his attention long, and self interest, at least in an economic sense, rarely affected his judgments. Certainly, he had an acute social conscience, and it was no whim that landed him on the side of revolution. But for Reed, it was the aesthetics of the matter, politics as poetry and theater, that compelled his attention.

There were two parts to his quest. In the political arena, Reed would search for color, tension, and release, preferably spiced with a taste of danger. He would also be inclined to judge the results of political action—indeed, revolution itself—at least in part by the depth and intensity of art that issued from it. Both elements first appeared in connection with his father's struggle against the big timber interests. Here, there was plenty of drama: courtroom confrontations, late-night meetings, secret detectives and spies, revelations of wrongdoing by prominent people, threats of physical danger that led Francis Heney to carry a gun during the trials and that led C. J. to fear that violence might be done to his loved ones. By the time the excitement was over, the young man had a new hero, journalist Lincoln Steffens, who had covered the events for a national magazine. One result was a rave review in the *Harvard Monthly* of Steffens's book *The Upbuilders*, a collection of biographies of reform leaders. Characteristically, Reed viewed this work through his own prism, writing that the full Progressive mentality would only be realized when the movement "finally gave birth to a new and splendid national expression in art."[12]

To see radical movements as theater was not difficult. Reed was only one of many partisans to describe strikes and revolutions as morality plays, with bloated capitalists and their minions—the police, the national guard, or the army—on one side and the oppressed workers and their leaders on the other. In Paterson, he admired Haywood, Tresca, and Elizabeth Gurley Flynn for "the boldness of their dream," and depicted the strike as "drama, change, democracy on the march... a war of the people."[13] Mexico was even more colorful: Villa appeared as a kind of Robin Hood; peons and vaqueros delivered lines full of uncanny folk wisdom; and rag-tag armies moved through startling landscapes of barren desert and mountain beneath theatrically lit skies. At the time of the Bolshevik takeover, a Greek-tragedy feeling of fate pervaded Reed's prose. The revolution was "endowed with the patient inevitability of mounting sap in spring," and it came like the turning of a season, with "tempest and wind, and then... a rush of red blossoming."[14] Leaders like Lenin and Trotsky were able to survive only—and here the image shifts—by swimming successfully on a mighty tide they were unable to control.

The desire for revolutionary movements to give birth to new artistic visions was common enough among Bohemians and radicals. With Reed, as always, this desire included a personal as well as a social hope. His earliest writings as a teenager were tales of adventure; his last attempts, penned in a Finnish jail cell in 1920, were outlines for two novels: one set in the mythic realm of knights; the other, autobiographical. In the two intervening decades, he had come a long way from the world of Cedar Hill, through Bohemia to Russia. But the original impulse to be a creative writer, to assert the primacy of art over life, had never entirely faded—for all his involvements in organizing the CLP and activities as a member of the Comintern.

This duality suggests that for Reed, creation and social conscience were inextricably linked. His best stories and one-act plays —some written long before his initial involvement with the IWW— are critical views of city life. Full of immigrants, derelicts, corrupt cops, shopgirls, hustlers, hookers, and ward-heel politicians, they portray an urban landscape where joy is a fleeting emotion in a realm of exploitation and loneliness. Paterson provided another opportunity for transmuting radicalism into art. The pageant Reed wrote and directed, in which Wobblies reenacted their own roles in the strike, stirred some critics to envision a new, popular, revolutionary theater with the power to move the masses toward action.

Four years later, in the days after the Bolshevik takeover, Read had similar notions in mind. Learning that many Ukrainian officials were on strike, he put himself forth—half jokingly, to be sure —as potential Commissar of Art and Amusement for the region.

His aim was to "get up great pageants" and to sponsor festivals "with fireworks, orchestras, and plays in the squares and everybody participating."[15] In the winter of 1919-1920, when Russia was suffering civil war, famine, and epidemics, he took time to seek out the haunts of Moscow's avant-garde, where he met the explosive Vladimir Mayakovsky and the futurists and was impressed by their experimental graphics and poetry. He was equally pleased to visit a Prolet Cult Center, where artists worked communally during the day and, in the evenings, gave classes for workers. In this center, one found evidence of a new kind of art, one with a character all its own. Not quite knowing what to make of the work here, Reed described it in a single word, at once neutral and full of hope: "proletarian."[16]

That the grandson of Henry Green and the son of C. J. Reed should find promise in such a word says much about social change between 1900 and 1920. From Reed's viewpoint, it was a matter of reform not living up to a vision of hope for all people. In a world of crisis, Progressives seemed impotent, unwilling, or unable to hold to their ideals. His first hero, Roosevelt, disappointed him by an exclusively national view of reform, by racism exhibited in contempt for Mexicans, and by jingoism after 1914. Woodrow Wilson, whom Reed had once believed as high-minded a leader as America could produce, had led the nation to war and then had stifled dissent—including *The Masses*—with unprecedented ferocity. Even Lincoln Steffens, C. J.'s friend and Jack's longtime mentor, had refused to stand against hysteria after 1917, urging Reed to write against the war but not to publish. Abroad it was the same. In Mexico, Carranza was a reformer, but he showed little sympathy with the land hunger of the peons; in Europe, liberal and even socialist leaders had forsaken ideals to embrace war; in Russia, Kerensky, a Socialist who sounded more like a reformer, proved to be weak and vacillating, blind to both the acute suffering and the real movement of the revolutionary masses.

Had economic and political analysis been his basic approach, Reed might have blamed all this failure on the power of capital to shape history and control men's destinies. Instead, he found reform wanting on several grounds, and its political ineffectiveness was but the final failure that turned him into a revolutionary. New heroes—Haywood, Villa, Trotsky, Lenin—took the place of earlier ones, but none dislodged the memory of a father who had passed away before Jack's first involvements with the IWW. Even after 1912, Reed believed C. J.'s death to be an offshoot of the timber battles. His own end was a similarly oblique result of political struggle, and the timing and parallelism of both deaths is suggestive. At once able to fulfill C. J. and yet grow beyond the values of his father's world, Reed could repudiate reform doctrines without forsaking the memory of a man whose love and support had helped to launch him on such an impressive career.

When John Reed arrived in Manhattan to seek fame as a writer, it was with his parents' blessing. His father wrote to Lincoln Steffens, "He is a poet, I think; keep him singing."[17] The young man needed no encouragement. Not for the likes of him was life a sombre moral pilgrimage, a burden of weighty duties and obligations. His was always a poet's vision, a demand that experience continually burst through the confines of mundane reality. Something in Reed longed for heroism, and he was drawn to arenas laden with color, adventure, excitement, and danger. It was hardly his choice that in the early twentieth century, the realms of social and political deviance, of Bohemia and radicalism, were the most likely areas for such activity. Yet these, two, suited his character and temperament, his education and social conscience.

In the grandeur of aim, furor of activity, and breadth of accomplishment, Reed may be unusual, but everything he wanted and believed reflected the values of the Bohemian subculture to which he belonged. His generation was not simply reacting against a parental mentality, but against a larger cultural view—a system of beliefs and attitudes that came to reformers as part of their middle-class heritage. Transcending all political differences between Progressives and their conservative opponents was a common notion of psychological humanity, of the kind of self that was necessary for individual success and social progress. In part, a legacy of puritanism, this mindset had solidified during the revolutionary era, when, according to a recent historian, a fusion of "Protestant asceticism and republican theory" had saddled America with the belief that man "had to devote his life to work, frugality and sobriety, and to be the master of his passions and instinctual needs."[18] Such a character structure, reinforced by a Social Darwinian gloss, was still the middle-class ideal at the turn of this century. For males, it was expressed in a fear of the feminine, the emotional, the frivolous, the passive, the luxurious, and the artistic. Such qualities were deemed hindrances in the serious struggle for life, both individual and international, and were largely relegated to the female half of the population.

The limits of reform, seen through the life of Reed and his generation, were only partly political; more important was the cultural dimension, the psychic boundaries that reformers shared as part of their class. Reform is, after all, a movement within the bourgeois social order. Bounded by a belief in progress, industrial growth, and clock time, it is an attempt to make that order fair without, however, disturbing the institution of private property that Marxists see as creating the conditions of economic exploitation and—as an offshoot—psychological misery. Bohemia, or what might also be called the counterculture, is a thrust beyond industrialization, instrumental values, and clock time; it is an attempt to heighten the validity of the tactile, emotional, artistic, and sensual dimensions of life. Its aims are to deepen feeling and extend the potentialities for experience, to find alternative ways of measuring happiness, and to allow those measurements to arise from within the individual.

Serious folk may be inclined to judge Reed's Bohemians harshly. Among them are found no reasoned critiques of the social order; rather, we find the gut reactions of spoiled children wanting the world's goods and wanting them now. This, it may be argued, is unrealistic; worse, it is self-centered. But that is just the point. The products of a society in which the self was promoted as the highest locus of value, Bohemians like Reed developed themselves along lines undreamed of by their reformist parents. To refuse to accept life as gray, drab, and routine, and to attempt to make it more venturesome, aesthetic, colorful, passionate, and interesting, may be selfishness, but it is also possible to see such behavior as an unconscious kind of experiment for the benefit of all. It is a view that looks two ways: back to preindustrial times, before what Max Weber called the "iron cage" of industrialism and bureaucracy was fastened upon the bourgeois world; and to postindustrial society, when the cage may be open once again. Reed and his generation took strength from indulgent parents and created a commentary on middle-class reform. The startling social changes since their day reveal the United States as a society still attempting to assimilate the results of their experiments with life. It is no exaggeration to say that the criticism of the limits of reform implicit in John Reed's life is now applicable to our own lives.

NOTES

1. This essay derives from my book *Romantic Revolutionary: A Biography of John Reed* (New York: Knopf, 1975), though the seven years since its completion seem to have altered some aspects of my interpretation. For a full picture of Reed's life and times, readers may consult that work.

2. This essay is based upon a notion of contrasting world views, or mindsets, as they appear in two groups: one, referred to as "reformers" or "Progressives"; the other, called "Bohemians," "Reed's generation," or "Greenwich Villagers." Well aware of the imprecision of such rough labels, I am nonetheless willing to insist that they do in fact correspond to clusters of historical belief and behavior that the historian cannot avoid discussing without impoverishing our sense of life. However, I do not wish to be simplistic in my approach. Robert Wohl's study, *The Generation of 1914* (Cambridge: Harvard, 1979), brilliantly analyzes the phenomenon of generational thinking and provides sharp warnings against the potential pitfalls of such an approach.

Here, I have attempted to heed his words. Thus, by "Reed's generation," I certainly do not mean all those people of his age group alive at that time; rather, I am focusing on that subset of his generation we call "Bohemians"—the writers, artists, and intellectuals who moved to urban centers such as Greenwich Village and who saw themselves as a distinct cultural group. Though at odds on many issues, they did share certain assumptions about life that were quite distinct from normal middle-class views at the time. In referring to such views as those held by their parents, I do not mean to be taken literally. In Reed's case, though his father was a Progressive and many of his peers also came from reform-oriented families, there were also Bohemians as old as Reed's parents. The larger point is that, symbolically, reformers were the parents of radicals. They provided a family and social context—growing permissiveness in child-rearing and education and growing willingness to experiment with social institutions—in which radical notions began to flourish. The views espoused in Greenwich Village were part of a long-running assault on bourgeois life, the difference being that in Reed's generation, the scale became large enough to be an issue with which defenders of middle-class culture had to deal. That no person was a pure type is taken for granted, but the balance of beliefs—as in Reed and his parents—were preponderantly on one side or the other.

Expressed in print and behavior, this became part of a major cultural dialogue still in progress. Aside from my own biography of Reed, one may consult the following for aspects of this culture clash: Albert Parry, *Garrets and Pretenders: A History of Bohemianism in America* (New York: Dover, 1960); Allen Churchill, *The Improper Bohemians* (New York: E. P. Dutton, 1959); Gilman M. Ostrander, *American Civilization in the First Machine Age: 1890-1940* (New York: Harper and Row, 1972); Van Wyck Brooks, *The Confident Years: 1885-1915* (New York: E. P. Dutton, 1952); Daniel Aaron, *Writers on the Left* (New York: Harcourt, Brace and World, 1961); Henry May, *The End of American Innocence* (New York: Knopf, 1959); James Gilbert, *Writers and Partisans: A History of Literary Radicalism in America* (New York: John Wiley, 1968); Robert E. Humphrey, *Children of Fantasy: The First Rebels of Greenwich Village* (New York: John Wiley, 1978); and Richard Miller, *Bohemia: The Protoculture Then and Now* (Chicago: Nelson-Hall, 1977).

3. Walter Lippmann, "Legendary John Reed," *New Republic* 1 (Dec. 26, 1914): 15-16.

4. "The Harvard Renaissance," unpublished essay, John Reed MSS, Houghton Library, Harvard University, pp. 3-4. The most important of the new political groups at Harvard was the Socialist Club, where young Walter Lippmann held forth. Other organizations included the Social Politics Club, the Single Tax Club, the Harvard Men's League for Women's Suffrage, and the Anarchist Club.

5. *The Day in Bohemia* (New York: printed for the author, 1913).

6. Lippman to Reed, Mar. 25, 1914, Reed MSS.

7. Louis Untermeyer, *From Another World* (New York: Harcourt, Brace, 1939), p. 58.

8. "Introduction," unpublished, datelined Christiania, Mar. 18, 1918, Reed MSS. This was obviously an early attempt to begin what later became *Ten Days That Shook the World*.

9. Eadmonn MacAlpine to Granville Hicks, Dec. 26, 1937, in Hicks MSS, George Arents Research Library, Syracuse University.

10. The marriage, on November 9, 1917, in Peekskill, occurred just before Reed entered the hospital for a major kidney operation; the motivation seems largely to have been to assure that Louise Bryant would be his legal heir.

11. Entitled "Where the Heart Is," the story appeared in *The Masses* 4 (January 1913): 8-9, and is reprinted in John Reed, *Adventures of a Young Man* (San Francisco: City Lights, 1975), pp. 23-29.

12. Harvard *Monthly* 50 (March 1910):36-37.

13. "Almost Thirty," unpublished autobiographical sketch, Reed MSS. A somewhat-edited version appeared in *New Republic* 86 (Apr. 15, 1936):267-70.

14. "Introduction."

15. Albert Rhys Williams to Granville Hicks, n.d., Hicks MSS.

16. From "Russian Notebooks," remaining fragments of notebooks Reed carried in Russia, Reed MSS.

17. Quoted in Lincoln Steffens, "John Reed," *Freeman* 2 (Nov. 3, 1920):181.

18. Ronald T. Takaki, *Iron Cages: Race and Culture in Nineteenth Century America* (New York: Knopf, 1979), pp. 9, 10.

8

GEORGE MOWRY: A HISTORIAN OF REFORM

Keith M. Heim

A good deal may be deduced about a historian as an individual by the thoughtful and perceptive reading of his published writings, and this may be particularly true if the writer has contributed seminal works in his field of study, as George E. Mowry has done. Scholarly interpretations and conclusions, drawn from essentially raw data, almost inevitably must reflect the writer's character and background to some extent. Students, too, may come to have some insight into the character and makeup of a professor through his courses and seminars. Yet neither the reader nor the student can gain a complete view of a professor, and their perceptions are often flawed.

While these characterizations are probably true of any historian, it seems to me that in George Mowry's case, it is particularly important, in evaluating his career and his influence upon the discipline of history, to consider his personality and background—to consider the man himself. Professor Mowry's career in history and his considerable contributions to that field derived from a remarkably well-integrated and consistent set of personal and professional standards that were rooted solidly in his early years spent in the Midwest. Accordingly, I shall not deal in depth with his work on the Progressive era; rather, I shall attempt to give, from personal acquaintance and observation, a clear picture of the man, to show the consistency between George Mowry the individual and Professor Mowry the scholar and teacher.

I suppose I knew George Mowry about as well as did any of his students. As a "Mowry student" at Chapel Hill in the early 1970s, I knew him, as others did, through his published writings, his well-structured and thoughtful classroom lectures, the give-and-take of late afternoon seminars, conferences in his office, and friendly chats in the crowded corridors of the history building, Saunders Hall. And while these contacts afforded me the impression of a genial mentor, dedicated to his discipline and to the craft of teaching, a necessary "privateness" often seemed to obscure him as an individual from the student.

Living as a student in an apartment in Mowry's home on Farrington Road for four years, I had a unique opportunity to search out the personal qualities that combined to influence his career as a historian. The opportunities to get to know him were many, and I made the most of them: I intercepted him in his morning inspection of the bird feeder outside his study window to ask his opinion on a historical question I had encountered in my reading the night before. I stealthily pushed my cat "Lillian" out the furnace-room door to lure him for a midmorning chat about ESP or the stock market. I accompanied him on his early-evening walks down to the Sparrow Cemetery and back, discussing his boyhood in Washington, D.C., and in Ohio, the New Deal writers' projects, and last Saturday's Carolina football game.

Looking back on those days, I think what struck me most from those encounters and leisurely talks was the breadth of his intellectual interests and the balance and tolerance that marked his opinions—qualities that characterized his professional career as well. I often marvelled at his familiarity with subjects ranging from art and anthropology to psychology and zoology. They were not superficial acquaintances. He had obviously read extensively in these subjects, digesting them in a rather pragmatic way and bringing them to bear on the topic at hand. He seldom seemed to have an intellectual "axe" to grind, listening intently to my contributions to the conversation, offered sometimes, I am afraid, in a random, shotgun fashion. He instinctively spotted shoddy reasoning and ill-thought-out positions, gently asking questions and allowing me to shift ground, somewhat unconsciously, to a more tenable viewpoint.

He was willing to change positions himself if the proper evidence was produced, and he was more tolerant of the questioning of his own ideas than some of his students of the late 1960s might have imagined. He was unfailingly polite, even when I had obviously not done my "homework" before taking a position. I remember that during one of our evening walks down to the cemetery, not long after I moved into the apartment, I questioned an interpretation of twentieth-century history (I shall not be more explicit out of respect for my own feelings rather than for Professor Mowry's). I challenged the basis of that particular interpretation by taking issue with a definition. Although he surely must have given me a sideways glance or two, wondering at my boldness in dissenting without any weight of real evidence on my part, he considered my opinions carefully, reasoning on both sides to make sure in his own mind that he, himself, had considered all angles. At the end of our walk, he left me with the impression that while there might be some merit in my point of view, the topic deserved more study than I had given it. A few weeks later, when my progress through a reading list brought me to Mowry's own book on that very subject, I realized how foolhardy I had been and how lucky I was to have escaped so lightly from a venture into the unknown. Other established scholars who were more direct in their methods might have left me at the cemetery.

As the incident shows, George Mowry was not only fair-minded and tolerant but he was also personally kind—a quality that marked his personal relationships and his teaching as well. I recall well an incident that occurred not long after I came to Carolina. I was waiting outside his office in Saunders Hall, hoping to discuss my first seminar paper, when a young graduate student came out of his office looking somewhat distressed. I went into the office and sat in a chair beside his desk. He was silent for a few moments, and then he looked at me sadly and asked, "How do you tell a student that he doesn't have the ability to go on for a Master's degree?" It struck me that after more than thirty-five years of teaching, he had not yet been able to make perfunctory decisions in such matters. The personal element still mattered greatly to him.

Most of the more than fifty doctoral candidates that Mowry turned out from California to Carolina could, I am sure, cite instances of his kindness to them: a personal word in the hallway, an intercession with the departmental ogre, an invitation to dinner at his home, or a secret loan to tide a student over until a check came from home. These actions often provided the boost, tangible or intangible, that kept students going through the loneliness and discouragement that visit every graduate student.

As a close neighbor, I was the frequent recipient of the thoughtfulness of Professor Mowry and his wife, LaVerne, as well. A kindred spirit of rare quality who did much to further her husband's career, LaVerne Mowry had completed most of her work toward a doctorate in English before her marriage. Few scholars ever had so astute an editor and critic under the same roof as did George Mowry! She shared a wide range of interests with her husband, read critically in art and literature, and worked creatively in ceramics and other crafts. In the frequent spats between her cat "Vodka" and my own "Lillian," she was a patient and understanding referee. She was always ready with a kind word for me, and her support as a faithful friend was constant, even during her last years of ill health.

Perhaps a portion of the sympathetic understanding I often received from the Mowrys during my years of tutelage at Chapel Hill derived from our shared origins in the Midwest. I had grown up on a farm in Nebraska, while LaVerne came from Wisconsin, and George had spent a good bit of his youth in Ohio. I believe that much of his impatience with social and intellectual pretense and with bureaucratic solutions was based in an essentially midwestern outlook. Although he once remarked that he occupied middle ground, having been raised in the nation's capital and on an Ohio farm, having known both urban and rural America, I think that he fundamentally considered himself a midwesterner.[1]

Mowry was born September 5, 1909, in Washington, D.C., the family having moved there from Celina, Ohio, a short time before. His father, who had been a teaching principal in Celina, worked for the Adams Express Company. Although George recalled with nostalgia the early days on Dingledine Street, where the family lived, during our long evening walks, he spoke more frequently and fondly of the summers spent at his grandmother's farm at Lima, Ohio.

It was to Lima that the family returned a few years after George's birth, and he was graduated from high school there. From those days in Ohio, he knew firsthand of the isolation of rural society during the early part of this century, of the values of hard work and determination that had so recently made a wilderness bloom. And

if the Progressives, as many have pointed out, looked backward
longingly to a bucolic age, Mowry's own heart and intellect shared
the ambivalence, which sharpened his understanding of the essential dilemma they faced.

Mowry's familiarity with a variety of academic disciplines and
their tools of investigation, coupled with a unique understanding of
the human element, especially as it existed in the Midwest, uniquely
fitted him for his role as a pioneering historian of the Progressive
movement and, indeed, of the first half of the twentieth century.
When he wrote about the Ash Can School, he wrote as one familiar
with the Old Masters as well. When he wrote of the pragmatic leadership of Theodore Roosevelt, he wrote as a man suspicious of
ideologues, aware that "politics is the art of the possible." When
he wrote of the great stock market crash of 1929, he wrote as a man
with no little expertise in the workings of Wall Street. But he also
wrote as a man who, having gone out to face the world during the
depths of the Depression, understood the impact of the great financial crash upon the individual. He had read Horatio Alger and
was familiar with the McGuffey *Reader*, purveyors of the morals of
mainstream America and the work ethic, and he had talked with
farmers in the remote regions of Wisconsin and with laborers in
Ohio factories. Looking back, I think, to a rural America reminis-
cent of his youth, he understood its values and he understood in a
rather personal way the difficult accommodation progressivism (at
least, some of it) made with the new nationalism.

The uses of economic concentration and the bureaucratic state
to preserve democracy and expand social justice posed a dilemma
for the Progressive, as they do for us in the 1980s. For George
Mowry, I think, the problem has been more than an academic
abstraction. Probably his own dedication to individual freedom
and to its handmaiden, academic freedom, was part of his inheri-
tance from his father, a "political liberal" who had fought for
those values in the public-school system in Ohio.[2] If, as students of
the New Left thought in the late 1960s, he was a "conservative," he
merited the label in an earlier sense (the terms have now gone to
mush), in which one favored change if it respected the rights of the
individual and was made in an orderly fashion. His "organic" view
of history dictated that one had to find out why a fence had been
put up before one tore it down. He was highly suspicious of elites
who would govern and of mobs as well. I think he tended to be

somewhat pessimistic about the politics of the 1960s, holding a guarded view of the perfectibility of mankind. Suspicious of reformers and social tinkerers, he had seen Prohibition, that noble experiment, fail, and he had seen the hopes of the Progressives for an immediate millennium frustrated in the 1920s. Heaven on earth, when it came, would not come overnight, and it certainly would not come through violence or by government fiat.

I have alluded to his disdain for elites and social pretense, and I am reminded of two stories he liked to tell. In the first, a midwestern farmer sending his son off to the city to make his fortune gave him this bit of advice, "Remember, son, you are as good as any man, and no better." The second story, shared with me because of my own background, concerned his mentor, John D. Hicks. When Hicks was teaching at Nebraska, he was assigned to squire a visiting scholar from Harvard University around the campus and to escort him to a convocation at which the visitor was to be the featured speaker. The easterner lost no opportunity during his stay to "put down" midwestern culture to his host, noting the obvious superiority of Harvard over the "cow college" in Lincoln. Hicks bore the gratuitous comparisons in silence, but while the two were seated on stage awaiting the visitor's introduction as the speaker of the evening, the easterner, unable to resist one more remark, leaned over and whispered to him, "Tell me, Dr. Hicks, how far east do you have to go before you come to a decent library?" Hicks replied, "The British Museum." The obvious relish with which Mowry repeated the story was significant.

John Hicks influenced Mowry's decision to pursue graduate studies in American history at the University of Wisconsin upon his graduation from Miami of Ohio.[3] Mowry had read the recently published *The Populist Revolt* and admired it,[4] and when Hicks moved from Nebraska to Wisconsin, Mowry followed him there. At Madison, he roomed with fellow graduate student T. Harry Williams "for four abominable years," as he laughingly described it. In later years, when the two met at history conventions, a good deal of banter between the former roommates revealed the lifelong regard and affection that had developed between them.[5]

Mowry entered Wisconsin in 1932, in the depths of the Great Depression, and the roommates had to resort to cooperative arrangements to remain solvent. So poor were they that he had to share his good coat with Williams and another roommate, only one of them being able to go out on a date on a particular evening.[6] To help finance his studies, Mowry taught off-campus classes at sites around the state, often traveling as much as 600 miles in a day and returning exhausted in the early hours of the morning. During this period, he met LaVerne Raasch, a graduate student in English from Milwaukee who was also teaching in the extension divison of the university. They were married in 1937, a year before he finished his doctoral studies.

Professor Mowry's first teaching position was at the University of North Carolina at Chapel Hill, where he remained until 1942, LaVerne continuing her doctoral studies in English at nearby Duke University. At the outbreak of World War II, he went to Washington, D.C., to serve as a civilian specialist with the U.S. Army Quartermaster Corps and, later, with the office of the chairman of the War Production Board. One suspects that his impatience with bureaucracies had its origin, at least in part, in wartime Washington.

In the fall of 1944, he went to Mills College in California to become May Treat Morrison Professor of American History, a post he held with distinction until 1947. During that period, he published *Theodore Roosevelt and the Progressive Movement*, which was based upon his doctoral dissertation, and he did much of the research for *The California Progressives.*[7]

The Mowrys returned to the Midwest in 1947, when he became professor of history at the University of Iowa. There, the popular young couple immersed themselves in the social and cultural life of campus and town, and he remembered those years later as among the most pleasant he had spent. In 1950, however, he accepted a similar position at the University of California at Los Angeles, where he remained until 1967, serving also as chairman of the Department of History from 1955 to 1967 and dean of the Division of Social Sciences from 1959 to 1967. While at UCLA, he wrote *The Era of Theodore Roosevelt* and *The Urban Nation*. With John D. Hicks and Robert Burke, he wrote *The American Nation*, *The Federal Union*, and *A History of American Democracy.*[8] By then generally recognized as the foremost scholar on progressivism, he served as a visiting professor in American history at the Universities of Strasbourg and Rennes, at Hebrew University, and at Oxford University; in 1965, his colleagues honored him with the presidency of the Organization of American Historians.

Perhaps it was a feeling of nostalgia for the earlier, less hectic days at Chapel Hill that led Mowry to leave California to return to North Carolina in 1967 to accept the prestigious chair of William Rand Kenan Professor of History. After an absence of a quarter of a century, George and LaVerne took up the threads of friendships with a number of individuals they had known before—the Godfreys, the Leflers, the Greens, the Spearmans, and others—and settled down into an existence of smog-free air, traffic jams made critical only by the hyperbole of the impatient, the change of seasons in the wooded hills, and leisurely walks in the country. Here, he enjoyed closer contacts with students and colleagues in the small-town atmosphere. Continuing his research, he wrote in 1973 *Another Look at the Twentieth-Century South* and began an extensive investigation into the history of conservatism in the United States.[9]

Mowry's career, as we have seen, literally spanned the breadth of the United States, and his writings have blanketed the first half of this century. His work on the Progressives—setting up the "Progressive profile" and showing the discontinuity of the movement with the Populists despite the similarity of programs—employed the full range of his intellectual interests and spawned a generation of scholars who have expanded his thesis and pursued lines of investigation suggested by his work. Inevitably, as these investigations have continued, new scholars have differed with some of his conclusions. Using his Progressive profile as a point of departure, they have shown the movement to have been an extremely broad, varied, and complex one in which business tycoons and labor leaders carried the banners of reform along with the solid, well-to-do middle class. Indeed, so disparate were the reformers that some have questioned that the phenomena constituted a movement at all!

The Progressives, themselves, recognized the pluralistic nature of the reform impulse. Walter Weyl remarked in 1912 that reform was carried along divergent lines by people holding separate interests. Mowry, himself, was certainly aware of the difficulties in encompassing all the phenomena of the era into a single, meaningful framework. I think, however, that his work has weathered well: he has not claimed too much for the Progressive profile, and he would be the last to try to stretch the reformers—and certainly not Teddy Roosevelt—upon a Procrustean bed. He would also be the last to permit theses and theories to become personal matters, as some have, to be defended and jealously guarded. Dedicated, as I have indicated, to the historical profession and to the spirit of free inquiry, he has welcomed and encouraged the continued research that might develop new insights in the field. Contrary evidence, as I came to see on those walks down to the cemetery, has no personal identity and is received on its merits. What matters is that the truth be revealed.

Recently, I asked historian Thomas D. Clark about George Mowry. The Kentuckian replied incisively, "The thing that I remember most about George is his absolute integrity!" Integrity— yes, of course. But a flood of other qualities come to mind from those years at Chapel Hill: keen intellect, broad academic interests, insight, and balanced judgment—all essential to the historian and teacher. Yet, in George Mowry, one cannot separate those images from others, the qualities of humanity. His is an understanding of human nature at its best and worst; his is a personal sympathy for the people of the age about which he wrote. In his personal relationships, there is warmth, kindness, sincere interest, and a keen sense of humor.

That his students have chosen to honor him at his retirement from teaching is testimony, not only to the lasting contributions he has made to the profession they have chosen, but also to the high personal regard and deep affection in which we hold him. He cared deeply about all of us as future historians and as individuals. And the qualities that made him a first-rate neighbor and friend also made him a first-rate teacher and historian.

NOTES

1. John A. Garraty, *Interpreting American History: Conversations with Historians*, 2 vols. (London and New York, 1970), 2:105.

2. Robert S. Mowry to Keith M. Heim, June 9, 1980.

3. Of his undergraduate days at the Oxford, Ohio, institution, Mowry remembered best setting a fire under the door to the dormitory room of a music major too diligent for his tastes in the study of the tuba, a recollection he did not share with any of the student activists on the Carolina campus in the late 1960s.

4. John D. Hicks, *The Populist Revolt* (Minneapolis, 1931).

5. I remember Mowry's returning from a history convention and relating an encounter with his old friend. Williams, he said, rushed up to him at the hotel, looking like the cat that had just swallowed the canary. "Say, Mowry," he called out, "I've been looking for you! The other day after my

lecture on the Progressive movement, a student came up to me and said, 'Have you ever heard of this guy George Mowry?' I told him that I had heard of him, and he said, 'Well, I've been reading one of his books, and I think you ought to know that he's been stealing your stuff!' '' Mowry's unconcealed glee, one imagines, almost matched that of Williams.

6. Elston and Sue Hill to Keith M. Heim, April 4, 1980.

7. George E. Mowry, *Theodore Roosevelt and the Progressive Movement* (Madison, Wis., 1946); *The California Progressives* (Berkeley, Calif., 1951).

8. Ibid.; *The Era of Theodore Roosevelt and the Birth of Modern America, 1900-1912* (New York, 1958); *The Urban Nation* (New York, 1965); John D. Hicks, George E. Mowry, and Robert Burke, *The American Nation* (Boston, 1963); *The Federal Union* (Boston, 1964); and *A History of American Democracy* (Boston, 1956). Also appearing in this period, along with numerous articles and essays, was *The Twenties: Fords, Flappers and Fanatics* (Englewood Cliffs, N.J., 1963).

9. George E. Mowry, *Another Look at the Twentieth-Century South*, The Walter Lynwood Fleming Lectures in Southern History (Baton Rouge, La., 1973).

Photograph of George E. Mowry

INTERVIEW WITH GEORGE MOWRY

Atlanta, Georgia, November 12, 1980

David R. Colburn and George E. Pozzetta

P: We might just begin by asking you to chat a minute about your own educational background. Could you talk about what brought you to the study of history, and what brought you specifically to the study of the Progressive era?

M: I had a sophomore high-school history teacher who influenced me, and secondly, I had a sophomore teacher in college, William E. Smith, who, besides being something of a scholar, was also a great teacher, and he introduced me to the Populist revolt. That, in turn, introduced me to John D. Hicks. I went to Wisconsin to work under Hicks after reading his study on the Populists.

P: What was Hick's like as a teacher and a mentor?

M: An old friend of his at Northwestern, who'd been his roommate for three years as a graduate student, made this comment about Hicks. "It's impossible in life for an individual to exist with less human meanness." I suppose I learned more outside the classroom with Hicks than I did in the classroom. If John had a weakness, it was a weakness that almost forbade him to criticize individual people.

P: Was it John Hicks who put you on to progressivism and reform?

M: At one point, he asked all the people who were going to go ahead for a Ph.D. to propose two or three subjects for study. So I suggested to him that I work on Slippery Simon Cameron, the interlocutor between the Pennsylvania railroads and Lincoln's cabinet. He said, "You're dealing with a second-rate figure. Why don't you get a big subject?" I went home to think of big subjects, and I thought of the Progressive movement. As soon as I mentioned that, John said, "*Fine*, go ahead. That's big enough!"

C: What aspect of progressivism did your dissertation cover?

M: I was doing a study of middle western progressivism, and I had gone through a lot of the middle western newspapers which were at the Wisconsin Historical Library. In my fourth year, I had a traveling fellowship, so I wandered around the Middle West, in Dolliver's, Cummins's, and Platt's papers, and so on. Finally, I ended up at the Library of Congress. Fortunately, I met Dr. J. Franklin Jameson, who was in charge of the manuscript collection. I was never more impressed with an older man. He was in his seventies. He said, "You're working on the Progressive movement. Why don't you get into Roosevelt Papers?" I told him I hadn't any idea that they were open. He said, "I just got word from the family that they are open and you may use them if you like."

P: The flukes of the profession!

M: That's right. Being at the right place, at the right time, with the right people. So I started to work with the Roosevelt Papers and produced my doctor's thesis on Theodore Roosevelt and the Progressive movement.

P: Were you the first scholar to work through the Roosevelt Papers?

M: No, Henry Pringle had used them up until 1909, but I
    was the first scholar to have seen the papers after 1909.

C: When you left Wisconsin, did you go directly to Iowa?

M: No, I went to North Carolina. I stayed there for four
    years and spent two summers in the Library of Congress
    and two summers up in the Berkshire Hills polishing
    and extending my thesis. Then the war broke out, and I
    sent it to Wisconsin Press. They wanted me to redo
    some parts of it, so I did that in an army camp, at Camp
    Lee, Virginia. Working on that thing in the midst of an
    army camp was difficult. But I finally got it in, and it
    was published in 1946.

P: George, is there anything that might characterize your
    approach to research?

M: I wasn't taught much methodology, and what method-
    ology I used on my thesis and later in my publications
    was largely self-induced. I hope I grew a little over the
    years—instead of just doing massive research and trying
    to put everything in. The editor of Wisconsin Press
    taught me some things about methodology and much
    about writing. I suspect the primary influence on my
    own methodology was the influence of two people. One
    was Charles A. Beard and his quantitative study of the
    making of the Constitution, and secondly, my growing
    awareness of some of the ideas of Sigmund Freud. I
    began to look at the emotional and often unrecognized
    forces behind the spoken and written word. I don't say
    that I used Freud that precisely. But in *The California
    Progressives*, which, in many ways, I think, is my most
    scholarly book, I tried to use both Beard's quantitative
    method and some Freudian explanations of their moti-
    vations.

C: What is it about *The California Progressives* that makes
    it your ablest work?

M: Well, when I moved to California, I found out that the
    Progressives were very literate men, and they had kept

their papers, especially the leaders, and I tried to structure a group study of all the Progressives that I could
find. Many of them had left records and manuscripts.
From these I tried to build up a personal and group
typology of progressivism in California. I attempted to
find out precisely who they were, what their perceptions
about the existing state of society were, what was
bugging them, and what they hoped to accomplish by
all the oratorical and political activity that subsequently
issued from them. Some years later, I attempted to do
much the same for a national group, but with this
cardinal difference in my sample: in California, for a
time at least, I was dealing with nonofficeholders;
whereas in the nation, most of the people in the sample
were rather prominent state or federal officials. And I
should admit that my earlier California findings
probably created a built-in bias in my later work with
national personalities.

P: Now, I know that at least one criticism of this approach
is that the opponents of the Progressives often fit the
typology just as neatly as the Progressives themselves. Is
that an accurate description of the California experience?

M: No, because I studied a good many California conservatives, and I should say that there were two or three
demarkations between the Progressives and the conservative groups. In the first place, the Progressives were
youngsters, comparatively speaking. In the second place
(as I tried to work out by what rudimentary "count'em
and collect'em" method I employed to make some
generalizations about them), they were a group that
consisted largely of an old class in American history—
newspaper editors, lawyers who were not lawyers of
big corporations, etc.—the people who represented, I
presume, a class in America that had practically disappeared. There were individuals who were from the professions, and some were teachers. This group was unlike
a great many of the existing politicians in the State of
California who were tied in with the railroads or/and

the rising oil companies. They represented, it seemed to me, a sharp break with the traditional political leadership. The educational background of the Progressives marked them again as an upper-class group, since practically all of them, whether men or women, were college graduates. Since a college degree still generally implied a basic literacy and a respect for the decencies of civilization, past and present, this was culturally a very superior group. This wasn't true of a good many of the old bosses in California politics. Now, that may have been a function of the generation because of the different approaches to education beginning in the 1880s—and additionally, I thought I saw some rather remarkable cohesiveness among the Progressives in the nature of their religions, except for two Jewish persons. As an aside, if I were writing the history of the Progressive movement now, I would emphasize the contribution of the Jews in proportion to their numbers a little more, and also emphasize more the role of women, which I did not previously detect. The women were not major factors at firsthand in politics but at second- and third-hand in leading causes that were tangential to the period. Like the settlement houses? Not only with the settlements, but with children's rights, legislation covering hours of labor for women, and women's rights.

P: Much of our recent literature suggests that the Progressive movement seems to have been much more pervasive throughout American society than perhaps some early observers had envisioned. I wonder if you've had any reflections on the pervasiveness of the reform impetus durng these years.

M: Oh, I think it's true. I think it was such a wide movement! I think that the people of my own generation did not have the perspicacity necessary to see how widespread this was in so many ways. It wasn't necessarily liberal in some ways, but there was a general dissatisfaction throughout the United States, especially in the cities (but even in the countryside), as to the responses of government to the rapidly rising and changing society that we had. On the other hand, I know that a good many people would say that the conservatives were an important part of the Progressive movement, but I would still insist that this was a very peculiar time in America—a time when a particular strata of the American middle class took action. A great many wealthy men contributed to the Progressive movement and supported its reforms. Oftentimes, these were changes that the average businessman at the time would have been against. The income tax, for example, the direct election of United States senators, these were not consrvative *issues*. The change in the political atmosphere, it seems to me, represented a sharp demarkation from the past and a sharp demarkation from the conservative ideology.

Most Progressives, of course, had a large strain of Darwinianism in their thinking: notably, Theodore Roosevelt in foreign policy, where the ultimate determination was by force and the one quintessential good was to survive. But most especially in domestic affairs, that determinism was tinctured with a liberal dose of optimism and of the more humane part of the Christian ethic. Change the environment and one changed man toward a more benign and social fellow, [that] has been the premise on which much of modern reform has been anchored, except possibly in very recent years. Few Progressives, however, were to go as far with their determination as a Watson and a Skinner were to do in the future: to the point that individual man can be shaped into almost anything and, as a consequence, is not responsible for anything, save possibly for putting his name on a fraudulent report to the Internal Revenue Service. The still-virile element of nineteenth-century individualism and the persistent although diminishing quantum of the Christian ethic often presupposed a choice and a personal and individual responsibility for that election.

The generous Progressive estimate of his fellow creatures imparted to their politics, for a time at least, a willingness to support a radical democratization of the public process and humanitarian reform. Their support of giving the franchise to women, for the direct election of senators, the use of a primary for selection of presidential nominees and a great many local and state offices, and the more spotty adoption of the initiative referendum and recall looked toward an untrammelled democratic process. The genuinness of the often-repeated Progressive slogan that "the cure for democracy was more democracy" has to be evaluated, of course, in the light of the southern reactionary trend toward the black man, and the alleged reduction of power of recent immigrant groups in the North by the attack upon the ethnic machines and the installation of city managers in many urban communities. As for the humanitarian impulse, literally hundreds of local, state, and national statutes dotted the books, prescribing new building restrictions in the interest of health and safety, limiting the hours for women, the proscription of child labor, the protection of youthful criminals, the regulation and sometimes suppression of vice and addictive drugs, and that interesting but futile attempt to bar the internal consumption of alcohol.

C: What work remains for Progressive historians?

M: I think a very interesting part of Progressive history is still to come. When the quantifiers get to work to see what the voters did in mass, we will learn a great deal more. After all, we older historians used to look at national politics and write history through senators and congressmen. Some of the people of my generation turned their attention to the states, but they aslo talked about state leadership, and very few of us had the necessary tools and training to examine individual voting. It was almost impossible, without computers, to conduct careful analytical work on voter responses and to correlate these with the prevailing religious, ethnic, and economic situation at a particular time. I'm sure there's a lot of ethnic and cultural values at work that we did not see reflected simply because we didn't employ either the right tactics or equipment. After all, these new quantifying historians are doing for society what the new life sciences are doing for the body—with the electronic microscopes—they're looking at cells now.

P: The extreme microcosm in society?

M: That's right. And if you can get at the voters, then it seems to me that you can make some judgments about the Progressive movement that we were not able to do, and this will revise a lot of the old conclusions.

P: Do you have any criticism of this approach to history?

M: Well, it's one thing to look at how they voted, but another thing to say *why* they voted the way they did. We're still, of course, finding things out about the problem of why things act the way they do. Why is green, green instead of white? Scientists can describe the process, but they can't give the ultimate why. It seems to me that it's pretty much emotional and often irrational. My experience in the last election whan I went to the voting booth—first, deciding I wouldn't vote for president and ending up voting for John Anderson—is an example.

P: It's hard to wrestle those things to the ground when you're standing there trying to study them in the aggregate.

M: Yes, and more difficult when you are trying to study events of forty or fifty years ago.

C: In addition, if you know how the people voted, it still doesn't tell you what their elective leaders are likely to do in a particular situation.

M: That's right.

C: They can often go in an entirely different direction from what the voters intended.

M: That's right. Because the political process, irrespective of the so-called debates of candidates, now is a process of largely running on your own record or assaulting the record of the previous four years. It's not a process of debating the so-called immediate, hard issues which have appeared and will appear in the next four, six, eight years ahead. As a consequence of that, the voter is pretty much like a historian—dealing with things of the past instead of making decisions on the probabilities of the future.

P: We were talking a moment ago about the pervasiveness of the Progressive reform movement. Do you have any reflections on what the Progressive movement might have missed?

M: Oh, yes. One of them obviously was the deteriorating state of race relations. The query is, Why this backsliding? It was not only backsliding in the South but back-sliding in the North and the acceptance in the North of what the South was doing. I suspect that the North, and the reformers that had tried to support blacks in the South in the Civil War years (they and their descendents), were so troubled by the enormous amount of new migration in their immediate neighborhoods in the North that they lost that emotional capacity to empathize with blacks in the South. In other words, I assume that there was a transfer here of dislike from the cities, teeming with Jewish people, eastern and southern Europeans, to the problems of the South, to the point where a great many people began to sympathize with the southern whites. It's an interesting equation to trace the shift of empathy and the shift of dislike—or disinterest —let's say. The response of lower-middle and middle-class people in the North toward the new immigration, while it might have been muted, was, in a way, a response of the whites themselves to the blacks. Now, I know that there were people in the cities who were trying to ameliorate the conditions of these people, but also I'd suggest that the immediate, emotional response of the average middle-class citizen in the northern cities is [that] "they will be trouble for tomorrow and we ought to slam the doors." The response of the American laborers, in reality, was the cry of "we who got here first don't want you to come."

P: When I've looked at those issues, the amazing thing to me has been, not that restrictive legislation was passed, but that it took so long to be enacted.

M: There, I suppose, it was a matter of tradition.

P: There were countervailing pressures, of course.

M: Also, the local politicos in our big cities in the North resisted such changes. By the time the people got excited about this issue, a great many of the previous immigrants had risen to political power, and they approached the situation with, at worst, an ambivalent feeling. I don't know what the response of, let's say, an Irish politician in Boston or New York or an Irish policeman in New York would have been to the question, "What do we do with all these people arriving on our shores?" What his response would have been, at best, would be ambivalent.

P: Can we just cast the net out a little bit wider for a moment and perhaps look at the broad sweep of American history and the role that reform has played in it? Any historian who plys the trade knows, of course, that there have been recurrent outbursts of reform activity. What reflections might you have on the nature of American reform as an ongoing process?

M: Well, I would say that the end of reform movements can be viewed through the actions of political elites. It seems to me that progressivism as an aspect of American reform went down to defeat in the period 1916-1920 largely because the groups supporting the central issues had run out of what they thought were permissible reforms, that any more reforms would have curtailed the intellectual, cultural, and economic comfort of the majority of the voters.

P: So progressivism reached the edge of permissible turf at that point?

M: That's right. The reaction to that was a cynicism, in part, or a turning to conservatism, if they were practicing politicians, or a retreat into other things.

C: How about the overall impact of progressivism on twentieth-century American reform, especially the New Deal?

M: Professor Louis L. Gould has written that the Progressives, somewhere in the years between 1900-1920, aside from one obvious and glaring exception, raised practically every social, economic, and political question that has engrossed every major reform movement since, running through Franklin Roosevelt's New Deal to Johnson's Great Society. The Progressives were silent on the question of the rights of blacks. But on the regulation of business, the conservation of the country's resources, the securing of uncontaminated foods and correctly labelled drugs, the reform of the existing political structure, the securing of rights for women, the protection and the better education of children, the control of the addictive drug traffic—from the long list of present domestic issues, you name it—the Progressives debated the particular issues voluminously and legislated, if not too well, at least often. From the amplitude and intensity of the reform appetite, the period between 1900 and 1920 reminds one of the yeasty, pre-Civil War years, before the national debate was all but monopolized by the slavery question.

C: Let's shift focus for a moment. I would like to talk about graduate students. What did you try to do in your relationships with your graduate students?

M: I guess I rather tried to let them make their own decisions and use my own intervention as little as possible in making those decisions. I would suggest in a mild way if I thought they were making mistakes. I think the choice of subjects was critical. I wanted people to be interested in their topics. In many ways, it is like selecting a marriage partner: you are with it for the rest of your life.

C: Have you always insisted that your students work on something significant?

M: Yes. I suppose, in a way, if a person persisted in choosing a topic that was not significant, I lost my interest in him or her. On the other hand, if they did something that was major, they may have bitten off a good bit more than they could chew. I always felt that as one grows older, one cuts back on goals. In other words, the productive age—sixteen-thirty—should be the age of great aspirations. You realize that 99 percent of people never achieve what they want, but nevertheless, without those aspirations, they would never achieve what they should have.

C: I always thought that one of the great strengths you had as an advisor was the freedom you gave students to succeed or fail on their own without constant instruction or supervision.

M: Well, how does one know? After all, when you are dealing with graduate students, you are dealing with people who are the operating people of the next ten or twenty years. Very few of us in this world are privileged to be able to say that this will be important in the future and this will not be. The only time that I think I issued a negative fiat was with things that I thought were absolutely impossible to achieve—be it for lack of manuscripts or the lack of financial support. Primary research is expensive in terms of time, effort, and money.

C: Let me ask you one last question. What are your thoughts about the history profession and your participation in it?

M: I have one firm thought. If I had to do it all over again, I would do it much the same. There are some mistakes I made which I wouldn't do over, but as a profession, a life—like Chaucer's clerk—I would gladly teach and gladly write.

BIBLIOGRAPHIC ESSAY _____

This brief section is intended to outline the major interpretations that have shaped our understanding of progressivism and to suggest directions for further reading. Two indispensable starting points for anyone interested in more extensive examinations of the historical literature on the Progressive era are George Mowry's instructive pamphlet published by the American Historical Association, *The Progressive Era, 1900-1920: The Reform Persuasion* (1972), and Robert Wiebe's "The Progressive Years, 1900-1917," in *The Reinterpretation of American History and Culture*, ed. William H. Cartwright and Richard L. Watson, Jr. (1973).

Students interested in sampling from the writings of Progressives themselves have a wide variety of materials at their disposal. Muckrakers such as Upton Sinclair, Ida Tarbell, Lincoln Steffens, and David Graham Phillips, to name a few, wrote extensively about the ills affecting American society. An excellent anthology of their writings is found in Arthur and Lila Weinberg's *The Muckrakers* (1961), and in the shorter work by David M. Chalmers, *The Muckrake Years* (1974). Many of the leading figures of American society left memoirs, and these often provide unique perspectives on the Progressive years. Among the more revealing are Lincoln Steffens's *The Autobiography of Lincoln Steffens*, 2 vols. (1931); Samuel Gompers's *Seventy Years of Life and Labor: An Autobiography*, 2 vols. (1925); Morris Hillquit's *Loose Leaves from a Busy Life* (1934); and Jane Addams's *Twenty Years at Hull House* (1910). The finely crafted collection, *The Letters of Theodore Roosevelt*, 8 vols. (1951-1954), by Elting E. Morison and John M. Blum, eds., affords important insights into the man and the president. Other useful collections for the era are Walter Johnson, ed., *Selected Letters of William Allen White, 1899-1943* (1947); Arthur H. Darling, ed., *The Public Papers of Francis G. Newlands*, 2 vols. (1932);

and Arthur Link's masterful *Papers of Woodrow Wilson*, a project that will run to an estimated forty volumes.

The massive changes that occurred in American society during the Progressive years have generated an unusually large number of interpretive studies by historians. Among the earliest of these studies are those that discerned clear links with the agrarian reform movement of the 1890s. Russell B. Nye's thorough study, *Midwestern Progressive Politics: A Historical Study of Its Origins and Development, 1870-1950* (1951), documents such political, economic, and philosophical ties for that section of the nation. Other studies that also find an essential continuity of reform issues between the two periods include Gene O. Clanton's *Kansas Populism: Ideas and Men* (1969), and Roy V. Scott's *The Agrarian Movement in Illinois, 1800-1896* (1962). David P. Thelen's *The New Citizenship: Origins of Progressivism in Wisconsin, 1885-1900* (1972) illuminates the careers and motivations of reformers at work in that Progressive state. A look at the South, which addresses the same themes but comes to different conclusions, is contained in Sheldon Hackney's *Populism to Progressivism in Alabama* (1969). Two compelling intellectual histories that expand the borders of this debate, as well as many others, are Eric Goldman's *Rendezvous with Destiny* (1952), and Richard Hofstadter's imaginative *The Age of Reform from Bryan to Franklin D. Roosevelt* (1955). Hofstadter's book has served to place the entire Progressive movement in the context of the fundamental forces of urbanization and industrialization that transformed the American nation during this era, especially as these social alterations affected the middle class.

Other historians have continued to utilize this last theme in their efforts to understand the nature of progressivism. George Mowry's *The California Progressives* (1951) outlined a "Progressive profile," which defined those persons pursuing reform goals in California. He found that these men were urban-oriented, generally young, well educated, and solidly from the well-to-do middle class. These were the people, in the view of Hofstadter, who felt most threatened by the changes then gripping America, and they responded out of a "status anxiety." The broad reforms emanating from the era reflected their efforts to cope with the shifting tides of society in that time period. J. Joseph Huthmacher, in "Urban Liberalism in the Age of Reform," *Mississippi Valley Historical Review* 49 (1962):231-41, argues that the immigrant lower classes of the great cities—through machines such as Tammany Hall—gave important support to Progressive reforms. Arthur Mann's *Yankee Reforms in an Urban Age* (1954) also finds reform agendas originating in the city environment.

The shifting patterns of intellectual development have similarly occupied the attentions of historians. Indispensable as an overview of this topic are Henry S. Commager's *The American Mind: An Interpretation of American Thought and Character Since the 1880s* (1952), and Daniel Aaron's *Men of Good Hope* (1951). Morton G. White's *Social Thought in America:*

The Revolt Against Formalism (1949) relates brilliantly the work of John Dewey, Thorstein Veblen, Oliver Wendell Holmes, Jr., Charles Beard, and James Harvey Robinson to the development of Progressive thought. Lawrence Cremin's study *The Transformation of the School: Progressivism in American Education* (1961) documents the role played by education in the era. The changing interplay of attitudes and programs concerning poverty and the poor are explored in Allen F. Davis's *Spearheads for Reform: The Social Settlements and the Progressive Movement, 1890-1914* (1967); Roy Lubove's *The Progressives and the Slums* (1962) and *The Professional Altruist* (1965); and Robert Bremner's *From the Depths: The Discovery of Poverty in the United States* (1956). The ambivalent feelings that many Progressives had toward elements of the new immigration in America are traced and analyzed in John Higham's *Strangers in the Land: Patterns of American Nativism, 1860-1925* (1955).

The influence of modernity, as exemplified in such phenomena as the drive for effiency in all areas of life and the emergence of an impersonal, cosmopolitan society in twentieth-century America, formed the basis of several recent attempts to interpret the Progressive era. Samuel Hays's *The Response to Industrialism, 1885-1914* (1957) pointed to the fact that businessmen and other organizational experts often lobbied for changes as a way of buttressing their own positions in society. He has developed these themes further in *Conservation and the Gospel of Efficiency: The Progressive Conservation Movement, 1890-1920* (1959). Support for this position has come from Robert Wiebe's *Businessmen and Reform: A Study of the Progressive Movement* (1962), and Samuel Haber's *Efficiency and Uplift: Scientific Management in the Progressive Era* (1964). Bradley Robert Rice's *Progressive Cities: The Commission Government Movement in America, 1901-1920* (1977) analyzes one aspect of this drive toward effiiency (the adoption of the city-commission system of government) and concludes that the city commissions did not succeed well in their mission. Wiebe has taken much of this material and woven it together with other themes to produce a provocative synthesis, *The Search for Order, 1877-1920* (1968). Wiebe views the Progressive era as being only one aspect of a much wider pattern of change in American society. An older America based upon "island communities" and characterized by essentially rural, agricultural values gave way in the late nineteenth century to a more modern, industrial society. Wiebe believes that the transformation was accomplished after a quick collapse of the older America around 1900. The new technological and interdependent world that emerged necessitated new strategies to cope with the essential needs of society in the realms of thought, politics, work, and social attitudes. Thus, the Progressives were responding to those pressures in their efforts to alter America.

These views have not gone unchallenged. A group of New Left historians have come to vastly different conclusions about the nature of the Progressive era. As a rule, these scholars have found the narrow interests of large, corporate business organizations to be the moving force behind the "reforms" of the age. Gabriel Kolko's *The Triumph of Conservativism: A Reinterpretation of American History, 1900-1916* (1963) offers an early example of this approach. Kolko maintains that large businessmen utilized many reforms to serve their own needs for security and, in fact, emerged from the period in a more dominant position in society than they had occupied before. His later study, *Railroads and Regulation, 1877-1916* (1965), added additional detail to that thesis. James Weinstein's *The Corporate Ideal in the Liberal State: 1900-1918* (1968) has supplied fuel to this interperative battle by focusing on local and state reforms, where he finds a similar pattern of business control. Peter G. Filene shifted the debate to another plane. In "An Obituary for the 'Progressive Movement,'" *American Quarterly* 22 (1970):20-34, he claimed that there exists no unifying theme or principle to characterize the era, and suggested that historians need to search for other approaches to those years.

A galaxy of specialized studies have added insights into various aspects of the Progressive era, and they should be consulted accordingly. Two masterful overviews that can guide the search for themes and issues are George E. Mowry's *The Era of Theodore Roosevelt, 1900-1912* (1958), and Arthur S. Link's *Woodrow Wilson and the Progressive Era, 1910-1917* (1954). The same two men have provided excellent studies of the men as presidents: Mowry's *Theodore Roosevelt and the Progressive Movement* (1946), and Link's multivolume biography *Papers of Woodrow Wilson* (1947-). Readers should also be aware of John A. Garraty's *Right-Hand Man: The Life of George E. Perkins* (1960), and Henry R. Pringle's thorough *Life and Times of William Howard Taft*, 2 vols. (1939). The nature of America's business leaders is recounted in delightful fashion in Frederick Lewis Allen's *Lords of Creation* (1935), while Allan Nevins and Frank E. Hill outline in detail the career of one such giant, *Ford: The Times, the Man, the Company, 1865-1910* (1954). Louis D. Brandeis's contributions are explored in Alpheus T. Mason's *Brandeis: A Free Man's Life* (1946). Zane L. Miller casts his gaze to the municipal level to view the actions of an urban boss faced with the problems of growth and change in *Boss Cox's Cincinnati: Urban Politics in the Progressive Era* (1968).

The southern Progressive experience is covered in two excellent volumes: George Tindall's *The Emergence of the New South, 1913-1945* (1967), and C. Vann Woodward's *Origins of the New South, 1877-1913* (1951). The women's movement receives coverage in William O'Neill's *Everyone Was Brave: The Rise and Fall of Feminism in America* (1969), and Aileen Kraditor's *The Ideas of the Woman Suffrage Movement* (1965). The best available study of conservatives in the Progressive era remains Richard M. Abrams's *Conservatism in a Progressive Era: Massachusetts Politics, 1900-1912* (1964). Labor has benefited from David Brody's *Steelworkers in America: The Nonunion Era* (1960), and Melvin Dubofsky's *We Shall Be*

All: A History of the Industrial Workers of the World (1969). Students interested in tracing the patterns of progressivism in foreign policy should direct their attentions to William Appleman Williams's provocative *The Tragedy of American Diplomacy* (1959), and for a very different view, to George F. Kennan's *American Diplomacy, 1900-1950* (1951).

James H. Timberlake has fitted the drive for national Prohibition into the wider patterns of the age in *Prohibition and the Progressive Movement, 1900-1920* (1963), and two recent books explore issues surrounding the police and social justice: Sanford Unger's *FBI* (1975), and Jerold Auerback's *Unequal Justice* (1976). The alterations that reform assumed in the 1920s are clearly outlined in Paul Carter's *Another Part of the Twenties* (1977).

GEORGE E. MOWRY'S
PUBLICATIONS _____

BOOKS

American Society in a Changing World, with C. H. Pegg, et al. (New York: Crofts, 1942).

Theodore Roosevelt and the Progressive Movement, 3 editions (Madison, Wis.: University of Wisconsin, 1946). Reprinted, The American Century Series (New York: Hill and Wang, 1960).

The California Progressives (Berkeley, University of California Press, 1951). Reprinted by Quadrangle/New York Times Books, New York, 1963.

A Short History of American Democracy, 6 editions, with John D. Hicks, (Boston: Houghton Mifflin, 1956).

The Era of Theodore Roosevelt, 1900-1912, (New York and Hamish Hamilton, London: Harper & Row, 1958). Reprinted by Harper Torchbooks, New York, 1962.

The American Nation, 5 editions, with John D. Hicks and Robert E. Burke (Boston: Houghton Mifflin, 1963).

The Federal Union, 5 editions, with John D. Hicks and Robert E. Burke (Boston: Houghton Mifflin, 1964).

The Urban Nation, 1920-1960 (New York: Hill and Wang, 1965; London and Melbourne: MacMillan, 1967).

A History of American Democracy, with John D. Hicks and Robert E. Burke (Boston: Houghton Mifflin, 1970).

Another Look at the Twentieth-Century South (Baton Rouge, La.: Louisiana State University Press, 1973).

The Urban Nation, 1920-1980, with Blaine A. Brownell (New York: Hill and Wang, 1981).

BOOKS EDITED

The American Tradition, The Unpublished Papers of John D. Hicks (Boston: Houghton Mifflin, 1955).

The Treason of the Senate, with Judson Grenier (Chicago: Quadrangle Press, 1964).

The Twenties: Fords, Flappers and Fanatics, (Englewood Cliffs, N.J.: Prentice Hall, 1963). Reprinted by Peter Smith, Boston, 1963.

ARTICLES

"The First World War and American Democracy," in *War As a Social Institution*, ed. Jesse D. Clarkson and Thomas C. Cochran (New York: Columbia University Press, 1941).

"The California Progressive," in Edward N. Saveth *Understanding the American Past*, (Boston: Little, Brown, 1954). Reprinted in at least 32 publications.

"The Progressive Era, 1897-1917," in *Interpreting and Teaching American History*, 31st Yearbook, National Council for the Social Studies, 1961.

"Social Democracy, 1910-1918," in C. Vann Woodward, *The Comparative Approach to American History* (New York and London: Basic Books, 1968).

"The Progressive Movement," in John A. Garraty, *Interpreting American History: Conversations with Historians* (New York: Macmillan, 1970).

"The Election of 1912," in Arthur M. Schlesinger, Jr., *History of American Presidential Elections, 1789-1968* (New York: McGraw-Hill, 1971).

"The Progressive Parties of 1912-1924," in Arthur M. Schlesinger, Jr., *History of American Political Parties* (New York: McGraw-Hill, 1973).

"The Twenties: the Limits of Freedom," in *Problems in American History*, ed. R. W. Leopold et al. (Englewood Cliffs, N.J.: Prentice Hall, 1972).

"Politics and Progressivism," in *The American Destiny: Bicentennial History of the United States*, ed. Henry Commager, vol. 2, chap. 3, Danbury Press, 1976.

"Editorial Foreword" to Richard L. Watson, Jr., *The Development of National Power* (Boston: Houghton Mifflin, 1976).

1945-present. At least fifty articles in various reference books and encyclopedias, including the *Dictionary of American Biography, Encyclopaedia Britannica, Americana Chambers, Great Britain, Encyclopaedia of the Social Sciences*.

1937-present. Approximately 100 book reviews in *American Historical Review, Journal of American History, American Political Science Review, Mississippi Valley Historical Review, Journal of Southern History, New York Times, Saturday Review of Literature.*

INDEX

THE CONTRIBUTORS

BLAINE A. BROWNELL is professor of urban studies and history, dean and codirector of the Graduate School, and director of the UAB Center for International Programs at the University of Alabama in Birmingham. He also serves as editor of the *Journal of Urban History*. He is author of *The Urban Ethnos in the South, 1920-1930*, coauthor of *Urban America: From Downtown to No Town*, and coauthor, with George E. Mowry, of *The Urban Nation, 1920-1980*, 2d ed.

DAVID R. COLBURN is associate professor of history and chairman of the department at the University of Florida. His research interests include race relations, minorities, and politics in the twentieth century. He has edited, with George Pozzetta, *America and the New Ethnicity* (1978); authored, with Richard Scher, *Florida's Gubernatorial Politics in the Twentieth Century* (1980); and edited, with Elizabeth Jacoway, *The Southern Businessmen and Desegregation* (1982).

JUDSON A. GRENIER is professor of history at California State University, Dominguez Hills, where he served as first chairman of the department. He has published articles on California history in the Civil War and the Progressive period, and on American journalism, particularly the muckraking movement. He is coauthor of *The Rumble of California Politics* and *A History of the California State University*. To commemorate the Bicentennial, he headed a team of historians who produced *A Guide to Historic Places in Los Angeles*.

KEITH M. HEIM is associate professor and head of the Pogue Special Collections Library at Murray State University, having previously taught in the Department of History at the University of North Carolina at Chapel Hill. His principal research efforts have been directed toward a reexamination of the beginnings of the cold war, and the early formulation of Truman's foreign policy.

GEORGE E. POZZETTA is associate professor of history at the University of Florida. His principal research efforts have focused on the themes of immigration and ethnicity in American life. He has edited, with D. R. Colburn, *America and the New Ethnicity* (1978). His most recent publication is *Pane E. Lavoro: The Italian-American Working Class* (1980).

ROBERT A. ROSENSTONE is professor of history at the California Institute of Technology. He is a specialist in cultural and radical history and is particularly concerned with the connections between American political and artistic movements and their counterparts in Europe and Asia. The author of numerous articles, *Crusade of the Left: The Lincoln Battalion in the Spanish Civil War* and *Romantic Revolutionary: A Biography of John Reed*, he has served as historical consultant for "Reds," the motion picture based upon John Reed's life.

EDWINA C. SMITH has taught at the Kansas City Art Institute and at Texas Tech University. She is interested in American conservatism and Gilded Age politics and foreign policy, and has published on the southern response to American imperialism from 1898-1899.

ROBERT C. VITZ is associate professor of history at Northern Kentucky University, where he has taught for the past ten years. His principal research efforts have been in the area of American culture, and he has written articles on American art and music. He is currently completing a study of Cincinnati's cultural institutions.

DATE DUE
